What People Are Saying about Don Gossett's Ministry and Writings...

"Don Gossett is a mighty man of faith. We are to be powerhouses for God, and Don Gossett teaches you how."

—*Marilyn Hickey*
Marilyn Hickey Ministries

"Each of Don Gossett's books, which God placed into my hands, helped me to advance one step further in my divine destiny.... Whenever this man of God writes, I read.... My life is one testimony of his powerful and transforming ministry."

—*Senior Pastor Dr. Roge Abergel,*
World Harvest Church,
Van Nuys, California

"Don Gossett's teachings from the Word have truly revolutionized and shaped our lives and ministry. The victories and successes we have experienced are largely attributed to his impact on our lives."

—*Pastor Jim and Rosie Parker,*
Living Word Christian Center,
Spokane, Washington

THE POWER OF
YOUR WORDS

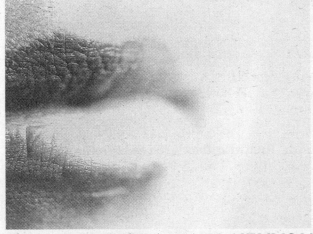

DON GOSSETT & E. W. KENYON

WHITAKER
HOUSE

Unless otherwise indicated, all Scripture quotations are taken from the King James Version (KJV) of the Holy Bible.

THE POWER OF YOUR WORDS
(previously published as *The Power of the Positive Confession of God's Word*)

Don Gossett
Bold Bible Missions
P.O. Box 2
Blaine, WA 98230
www.dongossett.com

ISBN: 978-0-88368-348-4
Printed in the United States of America
© 1977, 1981 by Don and Joyce Gossett

Whitaker House
1030 Hunt Valley Circle
New Kensington, PA 15068
www.whitakerhouse.com

19 20 21 22 23 24 **UJ** 16 15 14 13 12 11

Table of Contents

Introduction

For a long time I was confused over the fact that in my own life and the lives of others there was a continual sense of defeat and failure.

I prayed for the sick. I knew that the Bible was true, and I searched diligently to find the leakage.

One day I saw Hebrews 4:14, that we are to hold fast to our *confession* (*profession* in authorized version).

In the third chapter of Hebrews, I discovered that Christianity is called "The Great Confession."

I asked myself, "What confession am I to hold fast?"

I am to hold fast to my confession of the absolute integrity of the Bible.

I am to hold fast to the confession of the redemptive work of Christ.

I am to hold fast to my confession of the New Creation, of receiving the Life and Nature of God.

I am to hold fast to the confession that God is the strength of my life.

I am to hold fast to the confession that "Surely He hath borne my sicknesses and carried my diseases, and that by His stripes I am healed."

I found it very difficult to hold fast to the confession of perfect healing when I had pain in my body.

I made the discovery that I had been making two confessions. I had been confessing the absolute truthfulness of the Word of God, and at the same time I was making a confession that I was not healed.

If you had asked, "Do you believe that by His stripes you are healed?" I would have said, "Yes, sir, I do."

But in the next breath I would have said, "But the pain is still there." The second confession nullified the first.

In reality I had two confessions: first, a confession of my perfect healing and Redemption in Christ, and second, that the Redemption and healing was not a fact.

Then came the great battle to gain the mastery over my confession, until I learned to have but one confession.

If I confess that "My God shall supply every need of mine," I must not nullify that confession by saying, "Yes, God supplies my needs, but I cannot pay my rent, I cannot pay the telephone bill."

Faith holds fast to the confession of the Word.

Sense Knowledge holds fast to the confession of physical evidences.

If I accept Physical evidence against the Word of God, I nullify the Word as far as I am concerned.

But I hold fast to my confession that God's Word is true, that by His stripes I am healed, that My God does supply my needs.

I hold fast to that confession in the face of apparent contradictions, and He is bound to make good.

Many believers have failed when things become difficult because they lost their confession.

While the sun was shining brightly, their confessions were vigorous, strong and clear.

But when the storms came, the testings came, and the adversary was taking advantage of them, they gave up their testimony.

Every time that you confess disease and weakness and failure, you magnify the adversary above the Father, and you destroy your own confidence in the Word.

You are to hold fast to your confession in the face of apparent defeat.

You are to study the Word until you know what your rights are, and then hold fast to them.

Some make confessions without any foundations. Then the adversary whips and beats them badly.

You are to find out what your rights are. For instance, you know that He says, "Surely He hath borne our sicknesses and carried our diseases." Now you can make your confession.

"Nay, in all these things we are more than conquerors." There you can make your confession.

"Greater is he that is in me, than he that is in the world." You can make your confession here.

Stand by your confession through thick and thin, through good report and evil. You know that your confession is according to the Word.

Revelation 12:11, "And they overcame him because of the blood of the Lamb, and because of the word of their testimony."

E.W. Kenyon

Right and Wrong Confessions

F ew Christians have recognized the place that confession holds in the scheme of things. Whenever the word "confession" is used we instinctively think of confessing sin, weakness and failure. That is the negative side of this question.

Christianity is called "the Great Confession." Confessing is affirming something that we believe. It is testifying of something that we know. It is witnessing for a truth that we have embraced. Confession holds a very large place in Christianity.

Jesus planned that this great Life and Love should be given to the world through testimony, that is, through the confession of our lips. Testifiers and witnesses and confessors have been the great leaders in the revolutionary life that Jesus gave to the world. The major problem that we face then, is to know what we are to confess.

Our confession centers around several things: first, what God in Christ has wrought for us. Second, what God through the Word and the Spirit has wrought in us. Third, what we are to the Father in Christ. And last of all, what God can do through us, or what the Word will do in our lips.

You cannot confess or witness about things you do not know. It is what you have seen and heard that counts in the court room. It is what you know personally about Jesus Christ and about what you are in Christ that counts. How few of us dare to confess to the world what the Word declares that we are in Christ! Take this scripture: "Wherefore if any man is in Christ, he is a new creation" II Corinthians 5:17. What a revolutionary thing it would be for the Church to make a confession like that! They are not just forgiven sinners — not poor, weak, staggering, sinning church members. They are New Creations created in Christ Jesus with the life of God, the nature of God, and the ability of God in them.

What a stir it would make in the modern church for you to confess that you are absolutely redeemed. Ephesians 1:7-8, "In whom we have our redemption through His blood, the remission of our trespasses according to the riches of His grace, which He made to abound toward us in all wisdom and prudence."

That would mean that Satan's dominion has been broken, that he lost his dominion over your life the moment you became a new creation. You received a new Lord, Jesus Christ, to reign over you. Satan's dominion ended and Jesus' dominion began. Disease and sickness can no longer lord it over you. The old habits can no longer lord it over you. You are a new creation created in Christ.

What a stir there would be if this scripture became a reality, "Fear thou not, for I am with thee; be not dismayed, for I am thy God; I will strengthen thee; yea, I will help thee; yea I will uphold thee with the right hand of my righteousness."

"If God be for us, who can be against us?" That is the most revolutionary thing that has ever been taught. That is your confession as you stand before the world. "God is with me this morning."

I John 4:4, "Ye are of God, my little children, and have overcome them: because greater is He that is in you, than he that is in the world." You fearlessly say, "God is in me now; the Master of creation is in me!" What a confession that is!

You face life fearlessly. You know now that greater is He that is in you than all the forces that can be arrayed against you. You are facing bills that you cannot pay. You are facing enemies that you have no ability to conquer and yet you face them fearlessly.

You say with triumph, "He preparest a table before me in the presence of my enemies. He anoints my head with oil." I am filled with joy and victory because God has taken me over; He is fighting my battles."

I am not afraid of circumstances because "I can do all things in Him who strengthens me." He is not only my strength but He is at my right hand. He is my salvation; whom shall I fear? He throws light upon life's problems so that I know I can act intelligently. He is my salvation, my deliverance from every trap the enemy sets for me, from every snare in which he would enslave me. "God is the strength of my life, of whom shall I be afraid?" I am not afraid of anything. I have no fear because this God of Omnipotence is on my side. This is my continual confession.

I confess that I have a redemption that God planned and wrought in Christ.

I am a new creation of which He, Himself, is the Author and the Finisher.

I have a righteousness that permits me to stand in His presence as though sin had never been. I not only have righteousness reckoned to me but I have righteousness imparted to me in the new nature that I have received from Him. I have received His nature, His life; and in this life and nature is the Life of God. This makes me righteous even as He is righteous.

This is my confession. This gives me boldness in prayer. This builds faith. This makes my way sure. I am no longer hemmed in by limitations because I am united with the Limitless One.

He is the Vine and I am the branch. As a branch I bear His fruit because the Vine is imparting to me the fullness of His life. I know the reality of this because it has become a part of my very being.

I know I love because He has shed abroad His love in my heart through the Holy Spirit and I know that His nature in me is love. His love ability has gained the mastery for now I can love in whatever circumstances I am placed.

I can say with joy, "Sin shall not have dominion over me." It can no longer lord itself over me. Circumstances can no longer hold me in bondage and hinder my usefulness in the world. I have not only God's life in me and this great Spirit who raised up Jesus from the dead in me, but I have the use of Jesus' Name. He has given to me a legal right to use it. My confession is that whatever I ask of the Father in His Name, He gives to me. He has given me the power of attorney. I am using that power to help men. I am taking Jesus' place now. He is working His own work through me. He is living His own life in me.

Jesus said, "In my Name ye shall cast out demons." I am exercising my rights. He said, "In my Name ye shall lay hands on the sick and they shall recover." My hands become the medium through which His life pours. I am living the abundant life. I know my words are His words. His words broke the power of death, of demons, and healed the sick. They do the same things in my lips. This is my confession. This is my heart expressing itself through words in my lips. Confession is faith's way of expressing itself.

Faith, like love, is only revealed in action and word. There is no faith without confession. Faith grows with your confession. Confession does several things to the believer: It locates him. It fixes the landmarks of his life. It mightily affects his spirit, the inner man, when he makes his declaration. For instance, there is Romans 10:9-10, "That if thou shalt confess with thy mouth Jesus as Lord, and shalt believe in thy heart that God raised Him from the dead, thou shalt be saved: for with the heart man believeth unto righteousness; and with the mouth confession is made unto salvation."

There are two confessions involved here:

first, a confession of the Lordship of Jesus.
And second, that he has become the righteousness of God and is saved. These are positive
confessions. The reason that the majority of
Christians, though they are earnest, yet they
are weak, is because they have never dared
to make a confession of what they are in Christ.
What they must do is find what they are in
the mind of the Father—how He looks upon
them—and then confess it. This can be found
in the Epistles. When you find this, you boldly
make your confession of what the Word declares you are in Christ. As you do this, your
faith will abound. The reason your faith is
throttled and held in bondage is because you
have never dared to confess what God says
you are.

Remember that faith never grows beyond
your confession. Your daily confession of what
the Father is to you, what Jesus is now doing
for you at the right hand of the Father and
what the mighty Holy Spirit is doing in you
will build a positive, solid faith life. You will
not be afraid of any circumstance, of any disease, or of any condition. You will fearlessly
face life—a conqueror. After a while you will
find that Romans 8:37 is true, "Nay, in all
these things we are more than conquerors."
You will never be a conqueror until you confess
it.

A Wrong Confession

A wrong confession is the confession of defeat, failure, and of the supremacy of Satan. Talking about your combat with the devil, how he has hindered you and how he is holding you in bondage and keeping you sick is a confession of defeat. It is a wrong confession. It glorifies your adversary. It is an unconscious declaration that your Father-God is a failure. Most of the confessions that we hear today glorify the devil. It destroys faith and holds you in bondage.

The confession of your lips that has grown out of faith in your heart will absolutely defeat the adversary in every combat.

The confession of Satan's ability to hinder you and keep you from success, gives Satan dominion over you and fills you with fear and weakness. But if you boldly confess your Father's care and protection, and declare that He that is in you is greater than any force around you, you will rise above satanic influence.

Every time you confess your doubts and fears, you confess your weakness and your disease, you are openly confessing that the Word of God is not true and that God has failed to make it good. He declares that, "With His stripes you were healed," and, "Surely He hath borne our sicknesses and carried our diseases." Instead of confessing that He has borne my diseases and put them away, I confess that I still have them. I take the testimony of my senses instead of the testimony of the Word of God. As long as I hold fast to my confession of weakness, sickness, and pain, I will still have them. I may search for years for some man of God to pray the prayer of faith for me and it will be to no avail because my unbelief destroys the effect of his faith.

The believer who is always confessing his sins and his weaknesses is building weakness, failure and sin into his consciousness. If we do sin, when we confess it, He is faithful and righteous to forgive us and to cleanse us from all unrighteousness (I John 1:9). When that confession has been made, we never refer to it again. It is not past history because history can be remembered. This is as though it had never been. We should never remind ourselves or the Lord of our failings or of our past mistakes. They are not! If you confess anything, confess that you stand complete in Him—that what God has said in regard to your mistakes and blunders is absolutely true. We should never confess our sins to people. We may have to ask forgiveness of them, but then we are to forget it. Never tell anyone about your weakness or about your past blunders and failures. They will not forget them and some time will remind you of them. If you tell it to anyone, tell it to the Lord and then forget it.

Dare to Make Your Confession

You confess that God is the Lord of your life, that He is the Lord over disease, sickness and Satan. You hold fast to your confession of Jesus' absolute Lordship over everything that would keep you in bondage or hinder you from enjoying the finished work of Christ. In the face of every need, you confess that the Lord is your Shepherd. You do not want. (It is always in the present tense.) He is your supply. He is your health, your strength. He is the strength of your life; of whom will you be afraid?

Remember that we never realize beyond our confession. If you dare confess healing on the ground of the Word, then there is no sickness for you. In the face of pain and an open sore, you confess that with His stripes you are healed and you hold fast to your confession, never wavering, knowing that, "no Word from God is void of power."

The word "power" means "ability"—ability to make good. That Word will heal you if you continually confess it. Your body will respond to your mind and your spirit will gain the Lordship over your body and mind. Your body will obey your confession. "He sent His Word and healed them" Psalm 107:20. Jesus was that

Word. Now that Name of Jesus and the words of Jesus become your healing. Confession is confirming the Word of God. It is a confession of my confidence in what God has spoken.

Here are several confessions every believer should make: Romans 10:9-10, "That if thou shalt confess with thy mouth Jesus as Lord, and shalt believe in thy heart that God raised Him from the dead, thou shalt be saved: for with the heart man believeth unto righteousness; and with the mouth confession is made unto salvation." We confess the absolute Lordship of Jesus and the absolute righteousness that is imparted to us in our redemption. We dare to confess before the world and before the throne of God that Jesus is now our Lord and that we have received salvation and become the righteousness of God in Him. We confess that we are new creations of which Jesus is the Head and the Lord. The Word has taken Jesus' place in our lives. We are to obey the Word as we would obey Jesus if He stood in our presence.

A second confession is found in I Peter 5:7, "Casting all your anxiety upon Him, because He careth for you." We confess that we no longer have cares, anxieties, and burdens. We can never have prostration. We can never be unnerved and unfit for life's work. Our minds are complete and clear. Our spirits are free.

Our testimony has the unction of the Spirit upon it because He bears every burden, carries every load, and meets every need.

A third confession is, "The Lord is my Shepherd, I shall not want." I do not want for money. I do not want for health or rest. I do not want for strength. I do not want for anything. He is all that I need. This is a living reality. What a life is mine. What a sense of security, of power and of victory! You are not afraid to take your stand on Philippians 4:19, "My God shall supply every need of mine."

You loudly make your fourth confession, that Isaiah 53:3-5 is true. Every disease, every weakness and every infirmity was laid on Jesus Christ and you are free of them. Just as He bore your sin, He bore your disease. You stand complete in Him. Free from the burden, the power, the pain and the effect of disease. This confession gives you a healthy body, a clear mind and a conquering spirit.

Your fifth confession is that I Corinthians 1:30 is absolutely true, "But of Him are ye in Christ Jesus, who was made unto us wisdom from God and righteousness and sanctification and redemption." Christ has been made all these things unto you. You do not need to pray for wisdom as James tells the babes in Christ to do because He is your wisdom. You do not have to ask for righteousness because you have become the righteousness of God in Him. You don't have to ask Him to sanctify you because He is your sanctification. You do not have to pray for redemption because you are redeemed. He is your redemption. What a confession to make before the world!

Hebrews 4:14, "Let us hold fast our confession." We have found in a measure what our confession is, but there is a great deal more to it than you find in this book. Your success and usefulness in the world is going to be measured by your confession and by the tenacity with which you hold fast to that confession under all circumstances or the opinions of men. You will never yield to fear or listen to the voice of the senses. You stand by your confession knowing that God cannot fail you.

There is grave danger of a dual confession. You confess His faithfulness, the absolute faithfulness of His Word, yet at the same time you confess your sickness.

You confess your weakness, your lack of money, your lack of ability.

You have confessed that He was your supply, that He was your Healer. You have confessed that you were healed by His stripes.

Now you talk about your lack of ability to do this or that because of your sickness. You cannot do the housework or go about your business because you are not able to do it.

Yet you have made your confession that He was the strength of your life and that with His stripes you were healed. Your confession of sickness and disease destroys what you are in Christ or what He is to you. This is one of the most dangerous of all confessions. You will find that you have been so carefully trained in the confession of wrong, of failure, of weakness, of sin, of sickness and of want that it will take a great deal of discipline through the Word to cure you of the habit.

Now you make your confession and stand by it.

What I Confess I Possess

I confess Jesus as my Lord (Romans 10:9-10), I possess salvation.

I confess "by His stripes I am healed" Isaiah 53:5, I possess healing.

I confess "the Son has made me free" John 8:36, I possess absolute freedom.

I confess "the love of God is shed abroad in my heart by the Holy Ghost" Romans 5:5, I possess the ability to love everyone.

I confess "the righteous are bold as a lion" Proverbs 28:1, I possess lion-hearted boldness in spiritual warfare.

I confess "He will never leave me nor forsake me" Hebrews 13:5-6, I possess the presence of God each step I take.

I confess "I am the redeemed of the Lord" Psalm 107:2, I possess redemption benefits every day.

I confess "the anointing of the Holy One abideth in me" I John 2:27, I possess yoke-destroying results by this anointing (Isaiah 10:27).

I confess "in the Name of Jesus I can cast out devils" Mark 16:17, I possess dynamic deliverances as a devil-master.

I confess "I lay my hands on the sick and they shall recover" Mark 16:18, I possess positive healings for the oppressed.

I confess "I am a branch of the Living Vine" John 15:5, I possess Vine-life wherever I go.

I confess "I am the righteousness of God in Christ" II Corinthians 5:21, I possess the ability to stand freely in God's holy presence, and in Satan's presence as a victor!

I confess "I am a temple of the living God" II Corinthians 6:16, I possess God dwelling in me, and walking in me!

I confess "my God shall supply all my need" Philippians 4:19, I possess the supply of every need.

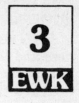

A Negative Confession

F ew of us realize that our confession imprisons us. The right kind of confession will set us free. It is not only our thinking; it is our words, our conversation, that build's power or weakness into us.

Our words are the coins in the Kingdom of Faith. Our words snare us and hold us in captivity or they set us free and become powerful in the lives of others. It is what we confess with our lips that really dominates our inner being. We unconsciously confess what we believe. If we talk sickness, it is because we believe in sickness. If we talk weakness and failure, it is because we believe in weakness and failure.

It is surprising what faith people have in wrong things. They firmly believe in cancer, ulcers of the stomach, tuberculosis and other incurable diseases. Their faith in that disease rises to the point where it utterly dominates them, rules them. They become absolute slaves.

They get the habit of confessing their weakness and their confession adds to the strength of their weakness. They confess their lack of faith and they are filled with doubts. They confess their fear and they become more fearful. They confess their fear of disease and the disease grows under the confession. They confess their lack and they build up a sense of lack which gains the supremacy in their lives.

When we realize that we will never rise above our confession, we are getting to the place where God can really begin to use us.

You confess that by His stripes you are healed; hold fast to your confession and no disease can stand before you.

Whether we realize it or not we are sowing words just as Jesus said in Luke 8:11, "The seed is the Word of God." The sower went forth to sow and the seed he was sowing was the Word of God. This is the seed we should sow. Others are sowing Sense Knowledge seeds of fear and doubt.

It is when we confess the Word of God, declare with emphasis that "by His stripes I am healed" or "my God supplies every need of mine" and hold fast to our confession that we see our deliverance.

Our words beget faith or doubt in others.

Revelation 12:11 declares, "And they overcame him because of the blood of the Lamb, and because of the word of their testimony." They overcame him with the Word of God that was in their testimony. They conquered the devil with words.

Most of the sick that Jesus healed during His ministry were healed with words. God created the universe with words: faith-filled words.

Jesus said, "Thy faith has made thee whole."

He said to dead Lazarus, "Come forth." His words raised the dead.

Satan is overcome by words, he is whipped by words.

Our lips become the means of transportation of God's deliverance from heaven to man's need here on earth. We use God's Word. We whisper "In Jesus' Name, demon come out of him." Jesus said, "In my Name ye shall cast out demons, in my Name ye shall lay hands on the sick and they shall recover." All with words!

Confession Precedes Possession

I confess, "For whosoever shall call upon the name of the Lord shall be saved" Romans 10:13, I possess know-so salvation for I have called upon the name of the Lord.

I confess, "The Lord shall preserve me from all evil" Psalm 121:7, I possess preservation from all forms of evil.

I confess, "Blessed are the pure in heart: for they shall see God" Matthew 5:8, I possess the assurance I shall see God, for the blood of Jesus has made me pure in heart.

I confess, "The Lord will give strength unto His people; the Lord will bless His people with peace" Psalm 29:11, I possess daily strength and an abundance of peace.

I confess, "Blessed be the Lord, who daily loadeth us with benefits" Psalm 68:19, I possess a life daily loaded with the benefits of the Lord.

I confess, "I am the light of the world: he that followeth Me shall not walk in darkness, but shall have the light of life" John 8:12, I possess light upon life's pathway for I am following Jesus.

I confess, "And God is able to make all grace abound toward you; that ye, always having all sufficiency in all things may abound to every good work" II Corinthians 9:8, I possess all grace, abounding grace—saving grace, healing grace, baptizing grace, all-sufficient grace.

I confess, "For with God nothing shall be impossible" Luke 1:37, I possess impossibilities becoming realities, for I am linked up with God by divine birth.

I confess, "I will pour out of my Spirit upon all flesh" Acts 2:17, I possess the Spirit outpoured upon my life continually.

I confess, "As far as the east is from the west, so far hath He removed our transgressions from us" Psalm 103:12, I possess the assurance that my sins are removed far from me, hallelujah!

Our Confession

Jesus evidently walked in the light of His confession.

He was what He confessed.

It is strange we never knew until recently that faith follows in the footprints of our confession.

Our confession builds the road over which faith hauls its mighty cargo.

You are going to learn that you never rise above your confession.

You will never enjoy the riches of grace until you confess them.

You are going to find that your confession of what He is, what He has done for you and what you are in Him, always precedes His revelation of Himself.

Salvation follows confession. "For if thou shalt confess with thy mouth Jesus as Lord."

And the same is true in receiving the Holy Spirit.

Our healing follows our confession.

Some people have to "hold fast to their confession" in the face of apparent defeat. They refuse to give in to sense evidences.

You are going to learn the danger of a dual confession; confessing one moment the absolute integrity of the Word but the next moment confessing that He has not made it good in your case.

Your confession is the thing that challenges the world.

It is the thing that causes them to venture in the faith life.

Christianity is the great confession.

It heads up in Jesus in His confession; and next in us in our bold declaration of the utter truthfulness of the living Word.

I Possess What I Confess

"With the mouth confession is made unto salvation" Romans 10:10.

I possess continual guidance for I confess "The Lord shall guide thee continually" Isaiah 58:11.

I possess eternal life for I confess "My sheep hear my voice and I give them eternal life" John 10:27.

I possess the peace of God for I confess "The peace of God which passeth all understanding, shall keep your hearts and minds through Christ Jesus our Lord" Philippians 4:7.

I possess freedom from fear for I confess "I the Lord thy God will hold thy right hand, saying unto thee, fear not" Isaiah 41:13.

I possess bountiful blessings financially for I confess "He which soweth bountifully shall reap also bountifully" II Corinthians 9:6.

I possess supernatural help in every situation for I confess "My help cometh from the Lord, which made heaven and earth" Psalm 121:2.

I possess good for I confess "Acquaint now thyself with Him, and be at peace: thereby good shall come unto thee" Job 22:21.

I possess peace with my enemies for I confess "When a man's ways please the Lord, He maketh even his enemies to be at peace with him" Proverbs 16:7.

I possess the ability to be a positive blessing for I confess "So will I save you, and ye shall be a blessing" Zechariah 8:13.

I possess wholesome, sound sleep at night for I confess "He giveth His beloved sleep" Psalm 127:2.

I possess the assurance my labour in the Lord is fruitful for I confess "Forasmuch as ye know that your labour is not in vain in the Lord" I Corinthians 15:58.

I possess as a faith man abounding blessings, for I confess "A faithful man shall abound with blessings" Proverbs 28:20.

I possess strength for my day for I confess "As thy days, so shall thy strength be" Deuteronomy 33:25.

I possess special honour from my Father for I confess "If any man serve Me, him will my Father honour" John 12:26.

The Place Confession Holds

T he Church has never given this vital subject
a place in its teaching and yet, answered
prayer, the use of Jesus' Name and faith are
utterly dependent upon it.

"Wherefore, holy brethren, partakers of the
heavenly calling, consider the Apostle and High
Priest of our confession" Hebrews 3:1.

Christianity is called our confession and in
Hebrews 4:14, He tells us to "hold fast our
confession."

The old version reads "profession," but the
Greek means witnessing a confession of our
lips.

You understand Romans 10:8-10, "That if
thou shalt confess with thy mouth Jesus as
Lord, and shalt believe in thine heart that God
raised Him from the dead, thou shalt be saved:
for with the heart man believeth unto righteousness; and with the mouth confession is

made unto salvation." You see the place that confession holds in salvation. It holds the same place in our faith walk.

Christianity is a Confession. It is our open confession of what we are in Christ, of what Christ is to us. Our faith is gauged by our confession. We never believe beyond our confession.

It is not a confession of sin; it is the confession of our place in Christ, of our legal rights, of what the Father has done for us in Christ and what the Spirit has done in us through the Word and what He is able to do through us.

There is a grave danger of our having two confessions. One would be the integrity of the Word and the other would be of our doubts and fears.

Every time we confess weakness and failure and doubt and fear, we go to the level of them.

We may pray very ardently and very earnestly and declare in our prayers our faith in the Word and yet, the next moment we question whether He heard us or not, for we confess we have not the things for which we prayed. Our last confession destroys our prayer.

One asked me to pray for his healing. I prayed for him and then he said, "I want you to keep on praying for me." I asked him what he wished me to pray for. He said, "Oh, for my healing." I said, "Prayer will be of no value. You have just denied the Word of God." The

Word says, "They that believe shall lay hands on the sick and they shall recover, and whatsoever ye shall ask in my Name, that will I do."

I prayed the prayer of faith and he denied it. By his confession, he annulled my prayer and destroyed the effect of my faith.

Your confession must absolutely agree with the Word and if you have prayed in Jesus' Name, you are to hold fast your confession. It is easy to destroy the effect of your prayer by a negative confession.

I Acknowledge

"Thy faith may become effectual by the acknowledging of every good thing which is in you in Christ Jesus" Philemon 6.

I acknowledge that "It is not I that live, but Christ liveth in me; and the life which I now live in the flesh, I live by the faith of the Son of God who loved me and gave Himself for me" Galatians 2:20. To acknowledge a fact is to confess that fact, to affirm it, to give testimony to it. Never can I forget the wonderful day when I walked up and down in my office affirming over and over, "Christ liveth in me!" And the life I now live, I live by the faith of the Son of God. It is His victorious faith by which I really live!

I acknowledge that "Now unto Him that is able to do exceeding abundantly above all that we ask or think, according to the power that worketh in us" Ephesians 3:20. In Christ that power is working within me. What is that power doing within? It is doing exceeding abundantly above all we can ask or think. Hallelujah. I acknowledge often that the power of God is working within me.

I acknowledge that "Whatsoever I ask the Father in Jesus' Name, He will give it to me" John 16:24. This is mine! Blessed privilege! Hallelujah! I ask the Father in Jesus' Name, and wonderful things happen. I acknowledge this fact.

I acknowledge that "Greater is He that is within me, than he that is in the world" I John 4:4. I constantly acknowledge that the Greater One is inside me. The Greater One has control of me and He is far greater than the enemy in this world. How dominant this makes me over adverse circumstances, problems, anxieties.

I acknowledge that "God hath not given me the spirit of fear, but of power, and of love, and of a sound mind" II Timothy 1:7. I acknowledge that within me is the spirit of power, of love and of a sound mind. This sets my faith on fire; I acknowledge that I have these right spirits of power, love, and a sound mind now.

I acknowledge that within me is liberty, for the Holy Spirit is within. "Now the Lord is that Spirit, and where the Spirit of the Lord is, there is liberty" II Corinthians 3:17. I never say, "I don't feel liberty within me." God says the Holy Spirit is within me, and because of that the mighty Holy Spirit that liberated from the dead the body of Jesus Christ indwelling me, that same mighty Spirit is producing liberty. I have the liberty of the Spirit; I am also a liberator, setting others free.

I acknowledge that "The love of God is shed abroad in my heart by the Holy Ghost" Romans 5:5. I acknowledge I can love with the same pure love with which Jesus loved needy humanity because the love of God is shed abroad in my heart. This is how I am known as a disciple of the Lord: "By this shall all men know that you are my disciples, if you have love one to another" John 13:35.

I acknowledge that "I can lay my hands on the sick and they shall recover" Mark 16:18. Jesus said so and it's my supernatural authority to administer His healing power to sick and infirm bodies. They shall recover.

9
EWK

The Two Confessions

After having prayed for one the other morning, she was satisfied that she was perfectly healed, but now the symptoms have returned and her heart is disturbed. She wonders where the difficulty lies.

I asked this party, "Did you tell your husband when you met him at night that you were healed?"

"No, you see I wasn't sure yet. I didn't want to say anything until I was positive."

"But you had no pain? Was there any soreness?" I asked.

"Oh, that all left; but you see I have to be careful. My husband is skeptical and I didn't want to tell him I was healed until I was sure."

I can see where her difficulty lay. She did not believe the Word. Had she made her confession to her husband, the thing would never have come back. But she played into the hands of the enemy, and he restored the same symptoms that she had had, and brought back the pain and soreness. This happened because she invited him to do it. Had she dared to stand her ground on the Word, and hold fast to her confession that she was healed, he would have no ground of approach.

Our faith or unbelief is determined by our confession. Few of us realize the effect of our spoken word on our own heart or on our adversary. He hears us make our confession of failure of sickness, or lack, and apparently he doesn't forget; and we unconsciously go down to the level of our confession. No one ever rises above it. If you confess sickness, it develops sickness in your system. If you confess doubt, the doubts become stronger. If you confess lack of finances, it stops the money from coming in. You say, "I can't understand this." No. Because most of us live in the sense realm and spiritual things are very indistinct.

Hebrews 4:14 must become a constant reality: "Having then a great high priest, who hath passed through the heavens, Jesus the Son of God, let us hold fast our confession." Our confession is that the Word cannot be broken; that what the Father says is true. When we doubt the Father, we are doubting His Word. When we doubt His Word, it is because we believe something else that is contrary to that

Word. Our confidence may be in the arm of flesh; it may be in medicine; it may be in institutions; but whatever our confidence is in, if it contradicts the Word, it destroys our faith life. It destroys our prayers. It brings us again into bondage.

Every person who walks by faith will have testings. They do not come from the Father; they come from the adversary. He is refusing to allow you to escape him. You become dangerous to the adversary when you become strong enough to resist him—when you have learned to trust in the ability of the Father to meet your every need. When that becomes a reality in your consciousness, the adversary is defeated.

But as long as he can confuse the issue and keep you in a state of flux, you are at a disadvantage. May your confidence in the Word be strengthened to make you know "that no Word from God is void of power" or can go by default. There isn't power in all the universe to void one statement of fact in this Word. He said, "I watch over my Word to perform it." And again, "Whosoever believeth on Him shall not be put to shame." Your confidence is in that unbroken, living Word, and you hold fast to your confession in the face of every assault of the enemy.

"These Things Affirm Constantly"

Titus 3:8

T he word confession in its positive meaning in the Bible is **affirming** what God has said in His Word. It is **witnessing** to the Word's declaration. It is **testifying** to truths revealed in the Book. We have been divinely instructed to "hold fast our confession" Hebrews 4:14 and again "let us hold fast the confession of our faith without wavering: (for He is faithful that promised)" Hebrews 10:23. Not only are we to hold fast our confession of the Word, but we are to affirm constantly those things God has revealed to us.

What is confession? Confession is saying what God has said in His Word about a certain thing. It is agreeing with God. It is saying the same thing the scripture says. To hold fast your confession is to say what God has said over and over until the thing desired in our heart and promised in the Word is fully manifested. There's no such thing as possession without confession.

When we discover our rights in Christ, we are to affirm these things constantly. Testify to them. Witness to these gigantic Bible facts. Or as Paul said in Philemon 6, "the communication of thy faith becomes effectual by the **acknowledging** of every good thing which is in you in Christ Jesus."

Affirmations of truth are to ring from our lips constantly. We are to hold fast to them without wavering. The penalty for wavering in our confession is that we deny ourselves God's Promise and the performance of it. "But let him ask in faith, nothing wavering. For he that wavereth . . . let not that man think he shall receive anything of the Lord" James 1:6-7.

"Let the redeemed of the Lord say so" Psalm 107:2. "Let such as love thy salvation say **continually**, let God be magnified" Psalm 70:4.

What things are we to affirm **constantly**? Affirm the positive scriptures that reveal the good things within us in Christ. There are hundreds of powerful affirmations to make constantly as we speak the language of the scripture.

These things affirm constantly:

> *God is who He says He is.*
> *I am who God says I am.*

God can do what He says He can do.
I can do what God says I can do.
God has what He says He has.
I have what God says I have.

11
EWK

Our Conversation

Few of us realize the effect that our conversations have upon our own spirits.

When you pretend to be what you are not and you talk glibly about it, it builds into your spirit a weakness. It is like a piece of rot in the beam of a building.

Or, your conversation may be full of discouragement, and you talk of your failures and inferiority. Eventually, it will rob you of initiative. You will find it difficult to rise above that mental attitude.

On the other hand, you speak the truth about what you are in Christ. You confess to your friends or your enemies what God is to you, and of your union with Him, and that you are actually partners with Him, that He is the One who backs you up and furnishes the capital to put the thing over. You give Him credit for His ability, for His wisdom, and you dare to make your confession boldly of your confidence in your success by His grace.

Jesus' bold and continual confession is our example. We are what He made us to be. Jesus confessed what He was. Sense Knowledge could not understand it. We are to confess what we are in Christ. Men of the senses will not understand us. To confess that you are redeemed, that your Redemption is an actual reality, that you are delivered out of Satan's dominion and authority, would be a daring confession to make. To confess that you are an actual New Creation created in Christ Jesus, that you are a partaker of the very nature and life of Deity, would amaze your friends. It isn't confessing it once, but daily affirming your relationship to Him, confessing your Righteousness, your ability to stand in His presence without the sense of guilt or inferiority.

Dare to stand in the presence of sense knowledge facts, and declare that you are what God says you are! For instance, sense knowledge declares that I am sick with an incurable disease. I confess that God laid that disease on Jesus and that Satan has no right to put it on me; that, "by His stripes I am healed." I am to hold fast to my confession in the face of apparent sense knowledge contradiction. Sense knowledge says that it is not true; that I am confessing an untruth. But I am confessing what God says.

You see, there are two kinds of truth: sense knowledge truth, and revelation truth; and they are usually opposed to each other. I live in the new realm above the senses, so I hold fast to my confession that I am what the Word says I am.

Suppose my senses have revealed the fact that I am in great need financially. The Word declares, ."My God shall supply every need of yours." I call His attention to what the senses have intimated, and He knows that my expectations are from Him. I refuse to be intimidated by sense evidences. I refuse to have my life governed by them. I know that greater is He that is in me than the forces that surround me. The forces that oppose me are in the senses. The power that is in me is the Holy Spirit; and I know that spiritual forces are greater than the forces in the sense realm. I maintain my confession of spiritual values, of spiritual realities in the face of sense contradictions.

Be Your Own Faith Builder

Don't dare read these paragraphs to follow quietly. They are only to be read aloud. You are building your own faith, for "faith cometh by hearing the Words of God." Go to it now, and be your own "Faith-Builder."

"I am a new creature in Christ Jesus. Yes, I am. What does this mean? It means that the moment I received Christ as my personal Saviour and Lord, I was born into God's royal family. I am a son of God. God has created me now in Christ Jesus. He has put new life into me. I have been born from above, born of the Spirit. Everything that God creates is good. I will not run down my life, because my life is in Christ. He made me, and not myself. I am what He has made me to be . . . A New Creature. I will not belittle myself, for I am in Christ, and in Christ I have been granted new life. The old life is gone. I am a citizen of a new kingdom. My citizenship is in Heaven.

"If you see an angel, ask him and he will tell you that my name is written down in Heaven. O wonder of wonders, I am a new creation in Christ. Created by God, His own workmanship. God is now working within me both to will and do of His own good pleasure. What is God doing within me? He is building me up! Making me strong in faith. How is He doing this? By His own Word!

"I am the righteousness of God in Christ. How do I know this? II Corinthians 5:21 is one of the great statements, among others, that tells me this fact. I am now righteous in Christ. Not only a new creature in Christ, but righteous in Christ. What does it mean to be righteous? It means that I possess the divine ability to be able to stand in God's holy presence without any sense of unworthiness. It means that God has made me righteous with His own righteousness. I stand before Him with no sense of unworthiness. So now that I am complete in Christ, I am free from that old inferiority complex that once held me captive. Hallelujah!

"I am redeemed from the kingdom of darkness and I have been translated into the Kingdom of God's dear Son. Once I was held in the realm of spiritual darkness. Satan was my lord and master. I was chained, bound, doomed for eternity in Hell. But then Jesus came and broke the bonds, loosed my soul from eternal damnation and gave me His life. I am now in that great kingdom where He reigns as Lord of lords and King of kings. He invites me to join Him right on the Throne. I reign with Him in life. Yes, I am redeemed. Once I lived in awful bondage to Satan. Sin was my master. I lived to gratify the flesh. But now in this new kingdom, sin has no dominion over me. In the old kingdom of darkness, I lived under the sway of sickness, fear, poverty and failure. I was held by unclean powers. But now through the blood of Jesus, I have been delivered. I say it boldly, "Goodbye sickness, goodbye fear, goodbye lack, goodbye weakness. I am free!" Now I live in a new kingdom, the heavenly kingdom where there is life, light, liberty, joy, peace, health, assurance, blessing and power. What a redemption is mine! What a Redeemer I have!

"I am an heir of God and a joint heir with Jesus Christ. To be saved isn't a light thing. I have received a rich inheritance. I am blessed with every spiritual blessing in the heavenly places in Christ Jesus. My Father loves me as He loved the Lord Jesus. My own wonderful Father is greater than all. He loves me with an everlasting love. Yes, I am blessed with heaven's best.

"My Christ said, 'I am the vine and ye are the branches.' That's how close I am linked with Him. He's that living Vine and I am a branch of that Vine. That same life, love, joy, peace, power, wisdom and ability that flows in the Vine flows into the branch. Wherever I, the branch go, the Vine-life flows!

"I have the life of God in my mortal body right now. Not just when I get to Heaven, but now, my spirit has been quickened, made alive and now I live and move and have my being in Christ. I have what God says I have. I can do what God says I can do. I am what God says I am.

"I _____, affirm that the above facts are forever settled in Heaven, and they are now settled in my heart. I shall often speak them boldly, and 'possess my possessions' in Christ Jesus."

Faith's Confession

Faith's confession is always a joyful confession. It confesses that we have the money before it has arrived. It confesses perfect healing while pain is still in the body. It confesses victory while defeat still holds it captive.

Your confession is based upon the living Word. "I know whom I have believed and am persuaded that He is not only able to make good, but He is making good now in my case."

I prayed for one who was very ill. After I had finished praying, the person said, "I know I am going to get well."

I knew that we were defeated, and I said to her, "When are you going to get well?"

She said, "I do not know when, but I know I will, for the Word cannot fail me."

I said, "No, but you have failed the Word. The Word is NOW, faith is NOW. Is the Word true in your case?"

She said, "Yes, indeed it is true."

"Then," I said, "by His stripes what?"

She saw it. "Why, by His stripes I am healed."

I said, "When?"

She said, "Now."

I said, "You had better get up and dress then."

I remember an aged man in Fredericton, New Brunswick, a deacon in the Baptist Church there, who came down with double pneumonia. Several of the local pastors and I went up to pray for him. I anointed him and we prayed. After we prayed, he said with a strong voice, "Wife, get my clothes, I am getting up." That was joy acting on the Word. When we confess the Word with joy, it brings conviction to the listeners. In Romans 10:10 it says, "For with the heart man believeth." I like to translate it like this, "For with the heart, man acts on the Word." The heart acts and that drives the lips to confession.

A doubting heart is a sense-ruled heart. A fearless confession comes from a Word-ruled heart. The Word dominates their heart life and they speak as did Paul, "I know whom I have believed."

As Paul stood on the deck of that ship in the midst of the awful storm, he said, "I believe God." Then he told those wondering men, "Every one of you will get to the shore safely, but the ship will be lost." He said, "Come, let us eat breakfast." He broke bread and gave thanks in the midst of them. He gave them more than bread, he gave them courage. Paul had a faith-filled, joyous confession. Only a heart that is nourished on the Word can stand in these hard places.

When we know that the Word is God speaking to us now, it is not difficult to act upon it. In the 82nd Psalm it declares that "the Word is settled in heaven." When I read that, I saw that it must be settled in my heart. I would no longer "try" to settle it. I knew that no Word from God was void of fulfillment. I was no longer afraid to act upon it.

The Word became more real to me than any word man had ever spoken. My lips were filled with laughter, my heart was filled with joy, and I had a victorious confession.

How many times have I seen the hesitant confession a forerunner of failure, and the joyful confession a forerunner of victory. When we fearlessly act upon the Word and joyfully cast our every care on Him, victory is as sure as the rising of the sun.

14

DG

Walking with God By Agreeing with God

How can I truly walk with God, unless I AGREE with God? To agree with God is to say the same thing God says in His Word about salvation, healing, answer to prayer and an overcoming life.

I agree with God that I am who God says I am: His heaven-born child. A new creature in Christ. More than a conqueror through Christ. I disagree with the devil who tells me I am "no-good," a failure, a weakling, that I am going under. I AGREE with God and disagree with the devil!

How may I walk with God in power, blessing and usefulness? By agreeing with God that I have what He says I have: His Name, His nature, His power, His authority, His love. I AGREE that I have what God says—in His Word—that I have!

"Enoch walked with God," and so do I by agreeing that I have received the ability to do what God says I can do: witness with power, cast out demons, minister His healing power. "I can do all things through Christ." I AGREE I can do what God says — in His Book — that I can do!

If I speak only what my senses dictate, I will not agree with God. It is speaking the "Word only" by which I agree with God. It is the "confession of faith" that is my victory.

To walk with God, I DISAGREE with the devil. Jesus did . . . by boldly declaring "it is written." I resist the devil by the Word.

Daily I walk with God by agreeing with God and His Word. "Because He hath said it . . . I may boldly say it" Hebrews 13:5-6.

Realization Follows Confession

We walk in the light of our testimony—our faith never goes beyond our confession.

The Word becomes real only as we confess its reality. The reason for this is, "we walk by faith and not by sight."

Sense knowledge would confess only what it had seen, heard or felt.

The people who are seeking experiences always walk by the senses.

Our testimony of the reality of the Word is feared by Satan.

"That if thou shalt confess with thy mouth." This reacts on our heart just as doubt spoken by the lips reacts on our heart.

You talk of your doubts and your fears, and you destroy your faith.

You talk of the ability of the Father that is yours, and fill your lips with praise for answers to prayers that you have asked. Its reaction upon the heart is tremendous: faith grows by leaps and bounds.

You talk about your trials and your difficulties, of your lack of faith, of your lack of money, and faith shrivels, loses its virility.

Your whole spirit life shrinks.

You study about what you are in Christ and then confess it boldly.

You dare to act on the Word in the face of sense knowledge opposition.

Regardless of appearance, you take your stand; make your confession and hold fast to it in the face of apparent impossibilities.

You see, faith doesn't ask for possible things. Faith is demanding the impossible.

Prayer is never for the possible, but always for the thing that is out of reason.

It is God who is at work with us, in us and for us.

"How shall he not with him freely give us all things?"

You see, you are launching out into the realm of the impossible just as Abraham did when he asked for a son.

You're not asking for something you can do for yourself, but for something that is beyond reason.

Then you refuse to take counsel with fear or to entertain a doubt.

The hardest battles I have ever fought have been along this line.

The greatest battles I have ever won have been those that seemed the most impossible, where there was the greatest opposition, where reason was discredited by faith.

I held fast to my confession and the Word was made good.

Confess your dominion over disease in Jesus' Name.

Never be frightened by any condition no matter how forbidding, how impossible the case may be.

It may be cancer, tuberculosis, or an accident in which death seems to be the master of the situation. You never give in.

You know you and God are masters of the situation.

You never for a moment lose your confession of your supremacy over the works of the adversary.

This disease, this calamity is not of God. It has but one source, Satan.

And in Jesus' Name, you are master. You have taken Jesus' place; you are acting in His stead.

You fearlessly take your position; confess your ability in Christ to meet any emergency.

Always remember that Jesus met defeat and conquered it. You are facing defeat everywhere as a master.

Don't let down. Keep your solid front.

Way's translation of Philippians 1:27-28: "Let your life as members of one communion be worthy of the glad tidings of the Messiah so that, whether I do come and see you, or whether I must still be afar and only hear news of you, I may know that with united soul you are working strenuously shoulder to shoulder for the faith of the glad tidings; may know that you are not cowed one whit by your adversaries. Their failure to daunt you is clear evidence— an actual sign from God— for them that their destruction is imminent; but for you, that salvation is yours."

That solid front spoken of in Colossians 2:5 (Weymouth), "Yet in spirit I am present with you, and am delighted to witness your good discipline and the solid front presented by your faith in Christ," is the solid front presented to your enemy.

You can't be conquered.

Your spirit is whispering, "Nay, in all these things I am more than a conqueror."

Every disease is of the adversary.

All kinds of sin are of the adversary.

All opposition to the glad tidings is of the adversary.

God and I are victors.

Greater is He that is in me than this opposition or this disease.

There is no need that is greater than my Lord.

There is no lack that He cannot meet.

This indomitable will that God has wrought in you cannot be overwhelmed, or conquered.

You remember what you are—you are a New Creation.

You are a branch of the Vine.

You are an heir of God.

You are united with Him. You and He are one; and He is the greater part of that one.

There is no such thing as conquering God when His instrument refuses to admit that the enemy can overwhelm him.

You are that instrument.

"I have learned in whatsoever state I am in, therein to be independent of circumstances" Philippians 4:11 *(Way)*.

Defeated with your Own Lips

You said that you could not, and the moment that you said it you were whipped.

You said you did not have faith, and doubt arose like a giant and bound you.

You are imprisoned with your own words.

You talked failure and failure held you in bondage.

Proverbs 6:2: "Thou art snared with the words of thy mouth."

Few of us realize that our words dominate us.

A young man said, "I was never whipped until I confessed I was whipped."

Another said, "The moment I began to make a bold, confident confession, a new courage that I had never known took possession of me."

Another young mother said, "My lips have been a constant curse. I have never been able to get the mastery of my lips."

A woman said the other day, "I always speak my mind." She has few friends. Only pity causes people to go see her. Her lips have been her curse.

It isn't so bad speaking your mind if you have the mind of Christ, but as long as you have a mind dominated by the devil, few people care to hear your mind.

Never fear failure.

Never talk defeat.

Never for a moment acknowledge that God's ability can't put you over.

Become "God-inside minded," remembering that greater is He that is in you than any force that can come against you; remembering that God created a universe with words; that words are more mighty than tanks or bombs, more mighty than the Army or Navy.

Learn to use words so they will work for you and be your servants.

Learn that your lips can make you a millionaire or a pauper; wanted or despised; a victor or a captive.

Your words can be filled with faith that will stir heaven and make men want you.

Remember that you can fill your words with love so they will melt the coldest heart, and warm and heal the broken and discouraged.

In other words, your words can become what you wish them to be.

You can make them rhyme. You can fill them with rhythm.

You can fill them with hatred, with poison; or you can make them breathe the very fragrance of heaven.

Now you can see vividly what your confession can mean to your own heart.

Your faith will never register above the words of your lips.

It isn't so bad to think a thing as it is to say it.

Thoughts may come and persist in staying, but you refuse to put them into words and they die unborn.

Cultivate the habit of thinking big things, and then learn to use words that will react upon your own spirit and make you a conqueror.

Jesus' confessions proved to be realities.

Faith's confessions create realities.

Jesus confessed that He was the Light of the world. He was it. The rejection of Him has plunged the world into a new darkness.

He said He was the Bread from heaven, and it is true. The people who have fed upon His words have never suffered want.

His words build faith as we act on them, let them live in us.

His words were filled with Himself; as we act on them, they fill us with Christ.

His words feed faith and cause it to grow in power in us.

The believer's words should be born of love and filled with love.

Our lips are taking the place of His.

Our words should never bruise or hurt, but should bless and heal.

Jesus was the Way, the Reality, and the Life.

We are taking His place, showing the Way, confessing the Reality, enjoying the Life.

You will never enjoy what you are in Christ until His love rules your lips.

16

DG

Don't Say "I Can't"
When God Says "You Can"

Don't say, "I can't." The phrase "I can't" is nowhere in the Bible. Speak God's language. Say what His Word says. Harmonize with heaven by affirming God's Word. Agree with God by agreeing with His Word.

Don't say, "I can't receive my healing." Boldly speak it, "**I can** receive my healing, for with His stripes I am healed. **I can** receive my healing because Jesus said they shall lay hands on the sick and they shall recover; hands have been laid upon me, thus I am recovering."

Don't say, "I can't pay my bills" Rather, declare it emphatically, "**I can** pay my bills," for my God shall supply all my need according to His riches in glory by Christ Jesus. I have honoured the Lord by paying my tithes and giving offerings in His Name, and He says He will open heaven's windows and pour me out overflowing blessings and will rebuke the devourer for my sake. **I can** pay my bills, because my God supplies the money to meet every need of my life."

Don't say, "I can't witness in power. I'm so weak and anemic as a Christian and when it comes to giving my testimony." Defeat that negative statement by affirming, "**I can** witness in power for I have received the Holy Spirit into my life, and Jesus said I would have power when I possess the mighty indwelling of the Holy Spirit. *I can* share my testimony, my witness for Christ, the message of His salvation with great effectiveness because I am energized by the mighty Holy Ghost from heaven."

Don't say, "I just can't get my prayers answered." This kind of expression will close the heavens to your life. With assurance, speak out, "**I can** receive the answer to my prayers, for Jesus said that whatsoever I ask the Father in His Name, He will give it to me. **I can** receive mighty answers from God, for He has promised if I would call unto Him, He would answer me and show me great and mighty things. I know **I can** receive the answer to my prayers, for this is my confidence in Him, that whatsoever I ask, I receive of Him, because I keep His commandments and do those things that are pleasing in His sight."

Don't say, "I can't see my loved ones won to

Jesus Christ." That's a lie of the devil, and for you to speak it is to give place to the devil. Agree with God's promise and declare it, **I can** see my loved ones all won to Jesus Christ, for God has promised that if I believe on the Lord Jesus Christ, not only would I be saved, but also, by believing, my whole household will be saved. I shall never fear that my loved ones will be lost forever in hell. **I can** see all my loved ones saved because I am God's instrument to believe for their salvation."

Don't say, "I can't overcome my overweight condition." Discover the ability of Christ by saying, "**I can** resist eating rich, fattening foods. Through the indwelling Christ, I can avoid high caloric foods. **I can**, by Christ's grace, overcome being a compulsive eater, and eat with moderation, temperance, for my belly shall not be my god. Hallelujah, I have discovered the secret: **I can** conquer my miserable overweight condition through Jesus Christ who is my strength and my sufficiency."

The Value of Confession

Realization can only follow confession. We walk in the light of our testimony.

The word becomes real only as we confess its reality.

Satan fears our testimony. If you confess something with your mouth, it reacts upon your heart or your spirit.

We confess what we are in Christ, then we act our confession.

If we confess our fears, they will rule us.

If we confess the dominion of disease, it asserts its lordship over our bodies more fully.

If we confess our freedom, that the Son has made us free, God makes that confession a reality.

When we realize that Jesus met defeat and conquered it, and we dare to make that confession, defeat and failure lose their dominion over us.

Thinking faith thoughts and speaking faith words leads the heart out of defeat into victory.

When we confess His Word, He watches over it to make it good, but there is no action on the part of God without our confession.

Christianity is called the "Great Confession."

Hebrews 3:1: "Consider the Apostle and High Priest of our confession, even Jesus." (Am. Rev.)

Hebrews 4:14: "Having then a great high priest, who hath passed through the heavens, Jesus the Son of God, let us hold fast our confession."

What is the confession to which we are to hold fast? That in Him we have a perfect redemption.

Colossions 1:13-14: "Who delivered us out of the authority of darkness, and translated us into the kingdom of the Son of His love; in whom we have our redemption, the remission of our sins."

That Redemption never becomes a reality until we confess it; few seem to grasp this fact.

In the face of apparent defeat, we confess our Redemption and deliverance, and it becomes a reality.

We do not ask for Redemption; we thank Him for it.

That Redemption was wrought according to I Peter 1:18-19, "Knowing that ye were redeemed, not with corruptible things, with silver or gold, from your vain manner of life handed down from your fathers; but with precious blood, as a lamb without blemish and without spot, even the blood of Christ." This is not a promise, but a fact.

Ephesians 2:10: we confess that we are New Creations, created in Christ Jesus, "For we are His workmanship, created in Christ Jesus for good works, which God afore prepared that we should walk in them."

II Corinthians 5:17: we dare to say, "Old things are passed away: behold all things are become new, all these things are of God, who reconciled us to Himself through Christ."

We know that we are not only redeemed and made New Creations, but that we are also reconciled. We dare confess it before the world.

We confess our Redemption from the hand of Satan, that he is unable to put disease upon us and hold us in bondage.

Revelations 12:11: "And they overcame him because of the blood of the lamb, and because of the word of their testimony."

The word here is *logos*. They overcame the adversary, because of the blood of the Lamb, and the *logos* that was in their testimony. They rested on the integrity of the Word.

They dared to confess that what God said was true.

Romans 4:25: "Who was delivered up for our trespasses, and was raised for our justification."

Romans 5:1: "Being therefore justified by faith, we have peace with God through our Lord Jesus Christ."

Then dare confess that this is true now.

Confess your righteousness in Christ.

We are now the Righteousness of God in Christ.

We dare declare this before the world.

We dare confess that God, Himself, has become our Righteousness. Romans 3:26.

We have been made by the New Birth and the Spirit, the very Righteousness of God in Him. "Him who knew no sin He made to be sin on our behalf; that we might become the Righteousness of God in Him" II Corinthians 5:21.

This is God's own declaration of what we are now; not what we want to be, but what God has made us to be.

I Peter 2:24 declares we are healed, "Who His own self bare our sins in His body upon the tree; that we, having died unto sins, might live unto righteousness; by whose stripes ye were healed."

The work is done.

It is not a problem of getting our healing, nor a problem of faith.

It is a problem of the integrity of the Word of God.

Can we depend upon that Word?

Jeremiah 1:12: "I watch over my Word to perform it."

Our confession must be a confession of the absolute faithfulness of the Word, of His finished work, and of the reality of our relationship as sons and daughters.

Our words determine our faith.

Our words are our confession.

If I continually confess lack; I believe in lack; my confession surely becomes a reality.

I confess the things which I believe.

If I believe in failure and weakness, I will confess it.

I will live up to the standard of my confession.

If I dare say that Psalm 34:10 is true, "But they that seek Jehovah shall not want any good thing," and if I stand by my confession, God will make good all I have confessed.

Psalm 84:11: "No good thing will He withhold from them that walk uprightly. O Jehovah of Hosts, blessed is the man that trusteth in thee."

I dare confess Proverbs 3:5, "Trust in Jehovah with all thy heart, and lean not upon thine own understanding: in all thy ways acknowledge Him, and He will direct thy paths."

That is guidance.

Not only is it deliverance from conditions, but it is a guidance into His will, into the paths of plenty.

Philippians 4:19 becomes the song of my heart, "And my God shall supply every need of yours according to His riches in glory in Christ Jesus."

What a confession this is. The heart waxes strong.

Isaiah 54:17: "No weapon that is formed against thee shall prosper; and every tongue that shall rise against thee in judgment thou shalt condemn. This is the heritage of the servants of Jehovah, and their righteousness which is of me saith Jehovah."

God is under obligation to stand by and care for His own. He cannot fail us.

Psalm 118:6: "Jehovah is on my side; I will not fear: What can man do unto me?"

Isaiah 41:10: "Fear thou not, for I am with thee; be not dismayed for I am thy God: I will strengthen thee; yea, I will help thee; yea, I will uphold thee with the right hand of my righteousness."

This is God's challenge, and I dare confess it before the world.

What a confession it makes!

God says to me personally: "Don't be afraid, child, I am with thee. Be not dismayed; I am your God."

He was Israel's God. Do you remember what happened to Pharoah and Egypt, and the Philistines? Exodus 14:21-31, I Samuel 14.

Do you remember what happened to all the nations that laid their hands upon Israel, while they were keeping the Covenant?

I Chronicles 16:22: "Touch not mine anointed ones."

He will take care of us as He took care of them. He will be our Protector and Caretaker.

Jesus said that faith would win. Faith has won. We are witnesses of this tremendous reality.

The Bible is God's confession. The more I read it, the more this great truth overshadows everything from Genesis to Revelation.

It is a continual confession of His greatness, His ability, His love, and His great Father heart.

Jesus, as you see Him in the four Gospels, is continually making confessions.

He is the Great Shepherd; He is the Light of the World.

John 10:11: "I am the good shepherd; the good shepherd layeth down his life for the sheep."

John 8:12: "I am the light of the world; he that followeth me shall not walk in the darkness, but shall have the light of life."

He said (John 14:6): "I am the way, and the truth and the life."

John 11:25: "I am the Resurrection and the life."

John 6:35: "I am the bread of life."

Those are tremendous confessions.

John 10:29: "My Father, who hath given them unto me, is greater than all; and no one is able to snatch them out of the Father's hand."

Jesus' confession led Him straight to Calvary.

John 5:18: "For this cause therefore the Jews sought the more to kill Him, because He not only breaks the sabbath, but he also called God his own Father, making Himself equal with God."

The fearless confessions of men down through the ages have given to us our martyrs.

Faith gives courage to confession, and confession gives boldness to faith.

Your confession lines you up, gives you your place, establishes your position.

We know what you are. If you are silent, we cannot place you.

Confession heals, or confession keeps you sick.

By your confession you are saved or lost.

By your confession, you have plenty, or you lack.

By your confession, you are weak, or you are strong.

You are what you confess with your lips, and what you believe in your heart.

Your confession of failure keeps you in the realm of failure.

Your confession of God's ability in your case, puts you over.

Proverbs 6:2: "Thou art snared with the words of thy mouth. Thou art taken with the words of thy mouth."

We are snared by our confession, or we are set free with the words of our confession.

Make your confession harmonize with the Word of God.

It will not harmonize with Sense Knowledge. Don't try to make it.

Sense knowledge calls it presumption or fanaticism, but God calls it faith and honors it.

Hebrews 11:1: "Now faith is assurance of things hoped for, a conviction of things not seen." God has done all that can be done for us.

He says that His Redemption is complete.

You confess that it is done, taking your place, calling yourself by the name that He has called you, acknowledging all the Word says is yours.

You now declare that all God has spoken, in your case is true.

John 8:32, 36: "And ye shall know the truth and the truth shall make you free."

"If therefore the Son shall make you free, ye shall be free indeed."

The truth will make you free. You declare that whom the Son has made free is free in reality, that sin cannot lord it over you any longer, that disease and sickness cannot lord it over you.

Romans 6:14: "For sin shall not have dominion over you," or "lord it over you."

Worry and anxiety cannot lord it over you. Satan's dominion is ended.

You stand complete in Him.

Few of us have realized the power of His Word on our lips.

He said in Mark 16:18 that those who believe "shall lay hands on the sick and they shall recover."

John 14:13: "Whatsoever ye shall ask (demand) in my Name, that will I do."

Acts 3 deals with the story of the Name in Peter's lips. He said, "look on us . . . In the Name of Jesus Christ of Nazareth, walk."

If you do not use the Name, the Name can do nothing.

But if you will use the Name, it will be as the Father's Name was in Jesus' lips.

In Acts 4:18-37 we are reminded of how the place was shaken by the name of Jesus.

18th verse, "and they called them, and charged them not to speak at all nor teach in the name of Jesus."

The Name in their lips had shaken Jerusalem to the foundation.

Acts 16:16-18 shows the power of the Name in Paul's lips.

He said, "I charge thee in the name of Jesus Christ to come out of her." She was healed and delivered.

John 15:7: "If ye abide in me, and my words abide in you, ask whatsoever you will, and it shall be done unto you."

The Word in your lips not only makes you free, but it sets others free.

The Word in your lips heals the sick.

The Word in your lips creates faith in the hearts of those who hear you.

The Word in your lips will change lives as they listen.

It is the very life of God in those words.

The Bible is God's Word.

In the lips of love and faith every Word is God-filled.

Our daily conversation is the Great Confession.

We confess Christ before the world.

We confess the fullness of His grace.

We confess the integrity of the Revelation.

Our first confession is Romans 10:9-10: "Because if thou shalt confess with thy mouth Jesus as Lord, and shalt believe in thy heart that God raised Him from the dead, thou shalt be saved: for with the heart man believeth unto righteousness; and with the mouth confession is made unto salvation."

We have found a perfect Redemption. We confess it to the world.

In Acts 10:36 Peter says, "He is Lord of All." How that thrills the heart.

He is the Lord of the three worlds: heaven, earth, and hell.

Every knee bows to that Name.

With joy we confess Psalm 23:1, "The Lord is my shepherd; I shall not want."

Jeremiah 16:19: "O Jehovah, my strength, and my stronghold, and my refuge in the day of affliction."

Philippians 4:13: "I can do all things in Christ who strengtheneth me."

I say to the world: "The Lord Jesus is my supply. He is my shepherd; I do not want."

There is a grave danger of our making a wrong confession, a wrong affirmation.

We confess our fears and doubts. That gives Satan dominion.

We confess our sickness and that confession binds our will as a captive and holds us in absolute slavery.

We confess want and lack of money, and want comes like an armed man and holds us in bondage.

We confess lack of ability, in the face of the fact that God said He was the strength of our life.

These confessions of failure shut the Father out, and let Satan in; give him the right-of-way.

These confessions repudiate the Word of God. They honor Satan.

What should we confess?

Psalm 23:1: "The Lord is my Shepherd; I do not want."

You are not afraid anymore, and you confess it.

John 10:29: "My Father is greater than all."

Our words imprison us, or they set us free. Our words put us in bondage, keep us from our freedom and our liberty in Christ.

Malachi 3:13: "Your words have been stout against me, saith Jehovah."

That is when our words war with His Word.

A woman came to me the other day. She said, "Mr. Kenyon, I have been prayed for, but I get no deliverance." Her word contradicted the Word of God.

His Word said, "If ye shall ask anything of the Father, He will give it you in my Name."

Mark 16:18: "They that believe . . . shall lay hands on the sick and they shall recover."

She repudiated it; she denied that the Word was true. Her words were warring against the Word of God.

She had unconsciously taken an attitude of mind that was against the Word.

She did not intend to, but she had done it.

That very attitude held her in bondage.

As I talked with her, I could see that she was not taking in what I said.

When I prayed for her, she was freed from pain, but the whine did not leave her voice. There was no confession of victory in her lips.

There is always a danger of a Mental Assent confession.

Mental Assent recognizes the truthfulness of the Word, but never acts upon it.

Its confession is: "Oh yes, there is healing in the Word. There is salvation and deliverance in the Word, but . . ."

On the other hand, faith joyfully confesses its victory. Its joy is a celebration; it is a triumph over the witnesses of the senses.

Faith gives a sense of security, of absolute assurance, of quietness and when this breaks forth in confession, it becomes a reality.

The heart must be rooted and grounded in the Word, and in love.

Acts 19:20: "So mightily grew the Word of the Lord and prevailed."

Faith is simply the Word prevailing over sense evidence.

Acts 20:32 gives us a striking illustration. "And now I commend you to God, and to the

Word of His grace, which is able to build you up and to give you the inheritance among all them that are sanctified."

It is the Word that establishes; it is the Word that builds.

It is the Word of His grace that builds faith into the heart of the believer.

Jesus' confession demands more careful attention.

John 5:19-20: Here are ten claims of Jesus. Everyone of them puts Him into the class of Deity. Read them carefully. Underscore them in your Bible.

John 5:43: "I came in my Father's Name."

John 5:46: "For if ye believed Moses, ye would believe me."

John 6:35: "I am the bread of life: he that cometh to me shall not hunger, and he that believeth on me shall never thirst."

This is a tremendous confession.

John 6:47: "He that believeth hath Eternal Life . . . I am the living bread which came down out of heaven."

John 7:29: "I know Him; because I am from Him, and He sent me."

John 8:29: "I do always the things that are pleasing to Him."

John 10:10: "I came that they may have Life, and may have it abundantly."

John 10:30: "I and the Father are one."

John 11:25: "I am the resurrection, and the life: he that believeth on me, though he die, yet shall he live."

These are a few of His confessions. Do we dare to confess what we are in Christ and what we have in Christ?

Dare we confess John 1:16? "Of His fulness have we all received, and grace upon grace."

We have received His fulness, but it has done us no good for we have failed to translate it into a confession.

Every believer knows that God laid his diseases on Jesus; yet he fears to make the confession and act on the Word.

This fear is of the adversary. It indicates that we have more confidence in the adversary than we have in the Word of God.

We confess that what He says is true.

Then we demonstrate it in our daily life.

There is no confession in the lives of many people.

There is much prayer, but there is no confession that the Word is true. It is not prayer many need, but confession of the Word.

I do not mean a confession of sin.

A woman said recently after I had prayed for her and opened the Word to her, "You will keep on praying for my disease, won't you?"

Her confession was that the Word was a lie.

You are to confess, that you can do what He says you can do, that you are what the Word says you are.

He says that you are a New Creation created in Christ Jesus.

He says that you are more than a victor; that you are an overcomer.

He made you to be a son, a daughter of God Almighty, an heir of God and a joint heir of Jesus Christ.

You can do all things in Him who is your strength. Philippians 4:13.

What He says I can do, I declare that I can do.

What He says I am, I declare that I am.

I make my confession boldly.

You make your confession: "God is my Father: I am His child. As a son in His family, I am taking my place. I am acting my part. I am in Christ. Christ is in me."

You remember that the Father will be to you what you confess Him to be.

If prayer is not answered, hold fast to your confession.

If the Name of Jesus does not give instant deliverance, hold fast your confession.

If the money does not come, stand by your confession.

Luke 1:37: "No Word from God is void of power."

Isaiah 55:11: The Word must accomplish the will of the Father.

"So shall my word be that goeth forth out of my mouth: it shall not return unto me void, but it shall accomplish that which I please, and it shall prosper in the thing whereto I sent it."

There is a danger of praying, then going back on your prayer.

When you pray for some need, and declare that the need is not met, you have repudiated your prayer.

But prayer is answered.

His Word is real.

Do not annul the Word by a negative confession.

Isaiah 41:10: "Fear thou not, for I am with thee; be not dismayed, for I am thy God; I will strengthen thee; yea, I will help thee; yea, I will uphold thee with the right hand of my Righteousness."

What I Am Not

I am not sick, for "my Lord healeth me of all my diseases" Psalm 103:3.

I am not bound, for "the Son has made me free" John 8:36.

I am not defeated, for "I'm more than a conqueror through Christ who loves me" Romans 8:37.

I am not weak, for "the Lord will give strength unto His people" Psalm 29:11.

I am not without power, for "ye shall receive power after that the Holy Ghost is come upon you" Acts 1:8.

I am not without peace, "being justified by faith, we have peace with God through our Lord Jesus Christ" Romans 5:1.

I am not lacking any good thing, for "no good thing will He withhold from them that walk uprightly" Psalm 84:11.

I am not overtaken by any evil work, for "the Lord shall deliver me from every evil work" II Timothy 4:18.

I am not afraid of any plague, for "there shall no evil befall thee, neither shall any plague come nigh thy dwelling" Psalm 91:10.

I am not running from the devil, for I am "resisting the devil, and he is fleeing from me" James 4:7.

I am not without daily quickening, for "He that raised up Christ from the dead shall also quicken your mortal bodies by His Spirit that dwelleth in you" Romans 8:11.

I am not shackled by sin, demons or fear; "thy God whom thou servest continually, He will deliver thee" Daniel 6:16.

I am not in a losing battle, "the Lord shall fight for me, and I shall hold my peace" Exodus 14:14.

I am not without joy; "His joy shall be in me, and my joy shall be full" John 15:11.

I shall not fail to see God; "blessed are the pure in heart for they shall see God" Matthew 5:8.

I am not oppressed by cares, difficulties and troubles; I am "casting all my cares upon Him, for He careth for me" I Peter 5:7.

Wrong Confession

Another desperate Enemy, and a persistent one, is Wrong Confession.

What do I mean by Wrong Confession?

You know that Christianity is really the Great Confession. Romans 10:9: "Because if thou shalt confess with thy mouth Jesus as Lord, and shalt believe in thy heart that God raised him from the dead, thou shalt be saved."

You notice it is a confession here with your lips.

(Whenever the word "Confession" is used we unconsciously think of sin. It is not confession of sin. It is a confession of our knowing that God's Son died for our sins according to Scripture, and that the third day He was raised again.)

Now, with my mouth I make confession of the Lordship of that raised One. I not only do that, but with my heart I have accepted His righteousness and I make confession of my Salvation.

You see there is no such thing as salvation without Confession.

So Hebrews 3:1 becomes clear: "Wherefore, holy brethren, partakers of a heavenly calling, consider the Apostle and High Priest of our confession, even Jesus."

You see, Christianity is our Confession.

In Hebrews 4:14 He says, "Let us hold fast our confession."

What is our Confession? Why, that God is our Father, we are His Children, we are in His Family.

It is a Confession that our Father knows what our needs are and has made provision to meet every one of them.

It is a Confession of the finished work of Christ, of what I am in Him, and what He is in me.

It is a Confession that "greater is He that is in me, than he that is in the world."

It is my Confession that my God does supply every need of mine according to His riches in glory.

It is my Confession that when I pray, the Father hears my prayer and answers me.

This is a manifold Confession.

If I were sick, I would maintain my Confession that "by His stripes I am healed."

If I were weak, I would insist upon this Confession that God is now "the strength of my life," and I can do all things in Him who is enabling me with His own ability.

If it is a problem of wisdom, I confess that Jesus has been made unto me Wisdom from God.

Here Are Some Don'ts

Don't try to believe, just act on the Word.

Don't have a double confession so that one moment you confess, "Yes, He heard my prayer I am healed," or "I will get the money," and then begin to question how it is going to come and what you ought to do to get it.

Your latter confession destroys prayer and destroys faith.

Don't trust in other people's faith—have your own.

Do your own believing. Have your own faith as you have your own clothes. Act on the Word for yourself.

Don't talk doubt or unbelief.

Never admit that you are a "Doubting Thomas;" that is an insult to your Father.

Don't talk about sickness and disease.

Never talk about failure. Talk about the Word, its absolute integrity, and of your utter confidence in it; of your ability to act on it; and hold fast to your confession of its truthfulness.

20

DG

What You Can Do

The secret of this message is to confess aloud each affirmation. Make it personal to your own life. Then you will be one of God's "used ones," that indomitable Christian who really gets things done . . . through Christ who indwells you.

"I can do all things through Christ which strengthens me" Philippians 4:13. The Bible is God's Word. When God says a thing, He means it. I can do what God says I can do!

Jesus said, "In my Name shall ye cast out devils . . . You shall lay hands on the sick and they shall recover" Mark 16:17-18. I can do that! In His Name I can cast out demons, and minister healing to the sick.

Psalms 37:4, "Delight thyself also in the Lord, and He shall give thee the desires of thine heart." I can have the desires of my heart, for I am delighting myself in the Lord!

Acts 1:8, "Ye shall receive power after that the Holy Ghost is come upon you, and ye shall be witnesses unto me." I can witness in power for I have the Holy Spirit in my life!

Isaiah 53:5, "With His stripes we are healed." I can possess healing and health for by His stripes I am healed!

John 13:34, "Love one another, as I have loved you." I can love others even as Jesus loved me, for His love is shed abroad in my heart. I love with His love!

I Corinthians 1:30, "Christ Jesus is made unto us wisdom from God." I can have divine wisdom in every crisis, for Christ Himself is my very wisdom.

Proverbs 28:1, "The righteous are bold as a lion." I can be bold as a lion, for I have been made righteous with His righteousness (Romans 10:10, II Corinthians 5:21).

Daniel 11:32, "And the people that do know their God shall be strong and do exploits." I can do exploits for I know my God Who makes me strong!

II Peter 1:3, "His divine power hath given us all things that pertain to life and godliness." I can enjoy ALL THINGS that pertain to both life and godliness, and I can do all things through Christ which strengtheneth me!

What I Confess, I Possess

It took me a long time to see this truth. After I saw it and thought I understood it, I still could not act upon it.

Christianity is called "the great confession." The law of that confession is that I confess I have a thing before I consciously possess it. Romans 10:9-10 gives you the law for entering the household of faith. "Because if thou shalt confess with thy mouth Jesus as Lord, and shalt believe in thy heart that God raised him from the dead, thou shalt be saved: for with the heart man believeth unto righteousness; and with the mouth confession is made unto salvation."

You see, with the heart man believes that Jesus is his Righteousness, and with his lips he makes a confession of his salvation.

You notice that confession of the lips comes before God acts upon our spirits and recreates them.

I say, "Jesus died for my sins according to scripture, and I now acknowledge Him as my Lord," and I know that the instant I acknowledge Him as my Lord I have Eternal Life.

I cannot have Eternal Life until I confess that I have it.

I confess that I have salvation before God acts and recreates me.

The same thing is true in regard to healing. I confess that "By His Stripes I am healed," and the disease is still in my body.

I say, "Surely He has borne my sicknesses and carried my pains and I have come to appreciate Him as the one who was stricken, smitten of God with my diseases, and now I know that by His stripes I am healed." (Lit. trans.)

I make the confession that "by His stripes I am healed;" the disease and its symptoms may not leave my body at once, but I hold fast to my confession.

I know that what He has said He is able to make good.

I know that I am healed because He said I was healed, and it makes no difference what the symptoms may be in my body. I laugh at them, and in the Name of Jesus I command the author of disease to leave my body.

He is defeated, and I am a victor.

I have learned this law, that when I boldly confess, then, and then only, do I possess.

I make my lips do their work. I give the Word its place. God has spoken, and I side with the Word.

If I side with the disease and the pain, there is no healing for me. But I take sides with the Word, and I repudiate the disease and sickness.

My confession gives me possession.

I want you to note this fact, faith is governed by our confession. If I say I have been prayed for and I am waiting now for God to heal me, I have repudiated my healing.

My confession should be this: the Word declares that I am healed, and I thank the Father for it, and I praise Him for it, because it is a fact.

You remember Philippians 4:6, 7: "In nothing be anxious; but in everything by prayer and supplication with thanksgiving let your requests be made known unto God. And the peace of God, which passeth all understanding, shall guard your hearts and your thoughts in Christ Jesus."

Why must prayer be made with thanksgiving? That means that I know the thing is done. I asked for it and now I have it, so I thank the Father for it.

The seventh verse says, "And the peace of God which passeth all understanding will fill my heart."

I am not worrying any longer. I have it. I am not *going* to get the money I need . . . I *have* it. It is just as real as though it were in my pocket. I am not *going* to get my healing . . . I *have* my healing because I have His Word, and my heart is filled with rapture.

Your confession solves the problem.

A wrong confession hinders the Spirit's work in your body. A neutral confession is unbelief. It is just as bad as a negative confession.

It is the positive, clear cut confession that wins.

"I know in whom I have believed."

"I know that no word from God is void of power or fulfillment."

"I know that He watches over His word to make it good."

These are the confessions of a victor.

I want you to notice several facts about the relation of confession to faith.

Your confession is your faith. If it be a neutral confession, you have neutral faith. If it is a negative confession, it is unbelief dominating your spirit.

Unbelief grows with a negative confession. A confession of failure puts failure on the throne. If I confess weakness, weakness dominates me. If I confess my sickness, I am held in bondage by it.

These negative confessions are acknowledgements of Satan's dominion over God's tabernacle.

Your spirit always responds to your confession.

Faith is not a product of the reasoning faculties, but of the recreated spirit.

When you were born again, you received the nature of the Father God. That nature grows in you with your acting on the Word, and your confession of the Father's perfect dominion in your body, and it causes your spirit to grow in grace and ability.

You remember that your confession is your present attitude toward the Father.

In some special testing that may come to you, your confession is either in the realm of faith or in the realm of unbelief. Your confession either honors the Father or Satan . . . either gives Satan or the Word dominance in your life.

Now you can see the value of holding fast to your confession.

Your confession either makes you a conqueror, or it defeats you. You rise or fall to the level of your confession.

Learn to hold fast to your confession in the hard places.

John 8:36, "If the Son has made you free you are free indeed." The Son has made you free, now stand fast in that liberty.

Galatians 5:1 is of vital importance to every believer. "For freedom did Christ set us free;

stand fast therefore."

The time to make your confession is when Satan attacks you. You feel the pain coming in your body. You repudiate it. You command it to leave in the Name of Jesus.

Romans 8:31-37, "If God is for us, who is against us?" Your Father is for you.

Disease cannot conquer you, nor can the author of disease. Circumstances cannot master you, because the Father and Jesus are greater than any circumstances.

You have learned that in whatsoever circumstance or condition you are, to rejoice in your continual victory.

You know that I John 4:4 is true. "Ye are of God, my little children, and have overcome them."

Notice who you are. "You are of God." "You are born of God." "You are a product of His, and of His own will He brought you forth through the Word."

The rest of the verse reads, "Greater is He that is in you than he that is in the world."

"For it is God who is at work within you, willing and working His own good pleasure."

Philippians 2:13 has been my victory many, many times.

Now turn to Romans 8:11, "But if the Spirit of Him that raised up Jesus from the dead dwelleth in you, He that raised up Christ Jesus from the dead shall give life also to your mortal bodies through His Spirit that dwelleth in you."

You must recognize this fact. All is yours by confession, or all is lost by a negative confession. You get God's best by the confession that you have it.

The secret of faith is the secret of confession.

Faith holds the confession that he has the thing he desires before he actually possesses it.

Sense Knowledge faith confesses that he is healed when the pain leaves and the swelling goes down. There is really no faith in that.

Faith declares you are healed while the pain is still wracking your body.

Let me state it again, possession comes with confession. Possession stays with continual confession.

You confess that you have it, and you thank the Father for it . . . then realization follows.

Remember, confession with thanksgiving always brings realization.

Confession is the melody of faith.

Confession before realization is foolishness to Sense Knowledge.

Abraham's faith was contrary to sense evidence. He waxed strong, giving glory to God, knowing that what God promised He would make good.

Sense Knowledge has no real faith in the Word.

John 17:23, "That they may know that thou lovest them even as thou lovest me."

Good Things in Me in Christ

"That the communication of thy faith may become effectual by the acknowledging of every good thing which is in you in Christ Jesus" Philemon 6.

God has shown me here a great faith secret: my faith will become effective (get things from God), by my acknowledging of every good thing which is in me in Christ Jesus.

Acknowledging is confessing or affirming the good things which are in me in Christ Jesus. This harmonizes with Romans 10:10—"What I confess I possess."

These good things I acknowledge that are within me, are not my own attainments, but what I have "in Christ Jesus." "All things are mine in Christ." "Of His fullness have I received."

One of the devil's subtle devices, of which I am not ignorant, lest he get an advantage of me, is to cause me to focus attention upon my past sins, my failures, my weaknesses, my mistakes. I will resist the devil and he will flee from me, by "thus saith the Lord."

My faith is set on fire, by acknowledging every good thing which is in me in Christ Jesus. It is acknowledging my possessions in Christ. What shall I acknowledge? That I am who God says I am. That I have what God says I have. That I can do what God says I can do!

I know that I go to the level of my confession. If it is a negative confession, acknowledging only the bad, rather than the "good things in me in Christ," I will go to the level of defeat, failure, weakness and lack. I refuse to do that! I shall acknowledge the GOOD THINGS I possess in Christ, and thereby my faith is dynamic, effective, on fire, gets things from God!

Effective faith I now have, by acknowledging every good thing in me in Christ Jesus! Hallelujah!

Some Facts about Affirmations

An affirmation is a statement of fact, or a supposed fact.

Faith and unbelief are built out of affirmations. The affirmation of a doubt builds unbelief. An affirmation of faith builds strength to believe more.

When you affirm that the Word of God cannot be broken, you affirm that the Word and God are one, that when you trust in the Word you are trusting in God the Father.

You affirm to your own heart that behind the Word is the throne of God, that the integrity of God in interwoven into the pattern of His Word.

Abraham counted that God was able to make good all that He promised.

God did make good on His promise to Abraham. The amazing thing is that He took a man one hundred years old and renewed his body, making it young again. He took a woman ninety years old and made her young, beautiful, and so attractive that a king fell in love with her.

She gave birth to a beautiful boy after she was ninety years old.

It was not Sarah's faith; it was Abraham's faith that made this woman young.

Doubt was a part of her life. She voiced her unbelief in a statement, and the angel heard her and reprimanded her for it (Genesis 18:12). She retreated in fear from the angel, as unbelief always makes us retreat.

When you constantly affirm that "Jesus is the Surety of the New Covenant" and that every word from Matthew to Revelation can be utterly depended upon, then that word in your lips is God speaking.

When you say what God told you to say, then it is as though Jesus was saying it.

When you remember that the Word never grows old, is never weak, never loses its power, but is always the living Word, the life-giving Word, and you boldly confess it, then it becomes a living thing in your lips.

When you confess that Satan has no ability to break the seal of the blood, and that "by the blood they overcame the adversary and by the Word of their testimony," you gain the ascendancy.

When you openly affirm His Word is what it confesses to be, the Word of God, that His Word is your contract as well as your contact with Him, then the Word becomes a living reality in your daily life.

Your word can become one with God's Word. His Word can become one with your word. His Word abiding in you gives you an authority in Heaven. That is a thrilling fact.

John 15:7 "If ye abide in me, and my words abide in you, ask whatsoever ye will, and it shall be done unto you."

The words of your lips are the words that abide in you and dominate you.

This visible Word gives faith in the unseen Word sitting at the right hand of God.

The Word you have in your hand carries you beyond Sense Knowledge, into the very presence of God, and gives you a standing there.

Right and Wrong Affirmations

We are continually affirming something, and that affirmation and the reactions of the affirmation upon our lives are sometimes very disastrous.

You know the effects the words of loved ones have upon you, well, the effect of your own words upon you is just as strong.

You continually say, "Well, I can't do it. I just can't do it. I haven't the strength to do it," and you feel your physical energy and your mental efficiency oozing away and leaving you weak and full of indecision and doubt, and your efficiency is gone.

You see, an affirmation is the expression of our faith: whether we have faith in ourselves, in loved ones, in the Bible or its Author; or whether we have faith in disease, failure and weakness.

Some people are always confessing their faith in diseases, their faith in failure and calamity. You will hear them confessing that their children are disobedient and that their husband or wife is not doing what is right.

They constantly confess failure and doubts. They little realize that that confession robs them of their ability and efficiency.

They little realize that that confession can change the solid, hard road into a boggy, clogged mire, but it is true. The confession of weakness will bind and hold you in captivity.

Talk poverty and you will have plenty of it. Confess your want, your lack of money all of the time, and you will always have a lack.

Your confession is the expression of your faith, and these confessions of lack and of sickness shut the Father God out of your life and let Satan in, giving him the right-of-way.

Confessions of failure give disease and failure dominion over your life. They honor Satan and rob God of His glory.

Here are a few good confessions: "The Lord is my Shepherd, I do not want." You say this in the face of the fact that want has been your master. A new Master has taken over the kingdom and you whisper it softly at first, "The Lord is my Shepherd," then you say it a little stronger; you keep repeating it until it dominates you.

When this becomes true in your life, you will never say again, "I want," or "I need," but you will say, "I have."

"He that believeth, hath." Believing is having.

Here you whisper, "My Father is greater than all." What a confession that is! My Father is greater than want, greater than disease, greater than weakness, greater than any enemy that can rise against me.

Then you say with deliberate confidence, "God is the strength of my life, of whom shall I be afraid?"

God is my strength. How much strength have I? God is the measure of it.

There are two types of affirmations that I wish you to notice. First, there is the affirmation with nothing behind it but my own will to make it good. It is based upon a philosophy born of Sense Knowledge. That Sense Knowledge is a product of my own mind. If it be in regard to sin, I deny the existence of it. If it be in regard to sickness, I deny that sickness has any existence. We see this in Christian Science.

If it is a problem of ability to meet a financial obligation, I affirm with all of my might that I have the ability to meet it.

All that I have to make these affirmations good is something that I am, or have, of myself. The Word of God has no place in this affirmation.

I cannot say that greater am I than disease, or greater am I than this demand upon me, consequently, my affirmation becomes a failure.

The second type of affirmation is based upon the Word of God.

The Word says, "If God be for you, who can be against you?" I know that He is for me. I know that this disease that was laid upon me has been defeated, that it was actually laid upon Christ, and "by His stripes I am healed."

That affirmation is based upon the Word of God, upon the Word that liveth and abideth and cannot be broken.

Jesus said, "Heaven and earth may pass away, but my Word will never pass away."

You see the vast difference between an affirmation based upon your own will or philosophy and an affirmation backed up by God Himself.

The affirmations based upon Sense Knowledge philosophy have no more value or ability to make good than is in the will and mind of the maker of the affirmation. But the affirmation that is based upon the living Word has God back of it to make it good.

Some Things that Are Not Faith

"Claiming the promises" is not faith. Faith already has it. "Claiming" proves that one does not have it yet. It is unbelief attempting to act like faith.

As long as one is trying to get it, faith has not yet acted. Faith says, "Thank you, Father." Faith has it. Faith has arrived. Faith stops praying and begins to praise.

Notice carefully, Doubt says, "I claim the promises." "I am standing on the promises." This is all the language of doubt.

Unbelief quotes the Word, but does not act upon it. We call this Mental Assent.

I can remember in those early days how we used to "plead the promises and claim them as ours." We did not know that our very language savored of unbelief.

You see, believing is simply acting on the Word. We act on the Word as we would act on the word of a loved one.

We act on the Word because we know that it is true. We do not try to believe it. We do not pray for faith, we simply act upon it.

One said to me the other day, "I am trying to make the Word true." I said, "I do not see why you need to do that, because it has always been true."

People do not know the Word until they begin to practice it and let it live in them. They may have sat under one of the finest teachers or preachers in the country for years, yet it has never become a part of their lives.

Using the Word in your daily life is the secret of faith.

The Word abides in you and enables Him to express Himself through you. You draw on the Vine-life for wisdom, love and ability. You are never without resources.

The Word is the Master speaking to you. When you act on the Word, you are acting in unison with Him. You and He are lifting the load together. He is fellowshipping with you, sharing with you. You are sharing His ability and strength.

Now you can understand that all that faith is is acting on the Word.

We are through with Sense Knowledge formulas.

Now we are walking with Him, realizing His ability has become ours.

Words that Work Wonders

"Whosoever offereth praise glorifieth me; and to him that ordereth his conversation aright will I shew the salvation of God" Psalm 50:23.

Words of praise glorify the Lord! I shall be a bold Praiser: one who praises the Lord. My resolve: "I will bless the Lord at all times; His praise shall continually be in my mouth" Psalm 34:1. As a Praiser, I extol the Lord, not so much for His gifts I receive, but I magnify the wonderful Giver Himself!

Words spoken in harmony with God's Word work wonders, too. I shall order my conversation aright. No "corrupt words shall proceed out of my mouth, but that which is good, to the use of edifying that it may minister grace to the hearers" Ephesians 4:29.

Words of confession of God's Word indeed work wonders. My confession always precedes my possession. The word "confession" means to say the same thing. I dare to say exactly what God says in His Word. I agree with God by speaking His Word in all circumstances.

How Can I:

Talk sickness when the Bible says, "With His stripes we are healed" Isaiah 53:5?

Talk weakness when the Bible says, "The Lord is the strength of my life" Psalm 27:1?

Talk defeat when the Bible says, "We are more than conquerors through Christ" Romans 8:37?

Talk lack when the Bible says, "My God shall supply all my need" Philippians 4:19?

Talk bondage when the Bible says, "The Son has made me free" John 8:36?

When I order my words aright, God manifests to me the benefits of His great salvation. "With the mouth confession is made unto salvation" Romans 10:10. With my mouth I make confession unto salvation, which includes healing, deliverance and every spiritual and physical blessing provided for us in Christ. By words I overcome Satan (Revelation 12:11).

I know also that words can work blunders. Most of our troubles are tongue troubles (Proverbs 21:23). A negative confession precedes possession of wrong things (Proverbs 6:2).

With the mouth confession can be made unto sickness, defeat, bondage, weakness, lack and failure. I refuse to have a bad confession.

My words work wonders. Words of praise. Words confessing God's Word. Words of bold authority expelling satanic power. Words of singing. Yes, words are the "coin of the kingdom." I boldly speak words that work wonders!

The Value of Confession

It is necessary that there be a continual confession of our redemption from Satan's dominion and that he no longer rules us with condemnation nor fear of disease.

We hold fast to this confession, as our confession is Satan's defeat.

We believers do not ask to be healed, because we have been healed.

We do not ask to be made Righteous, because we have been made Righteous.

We do not ask to be Redeemed, for our Redemption is an absolute fact.

In the mind of the Father, we are perfectly healed and perfectly free from sin, because He laid our diseases and our sins upon His Son.

His Son was made sin with our sins. He was made sick with our diseases.

In the mind of Christ, we are perfectly healed because He can remember when He was made sin with our sins, when He was made sick with our diseases. He remembers when He put our sin and our diseases away.

In the mind of the Holy Spirit we are absolutely free from both, for He remembers when Christ was made sin and when He was made sick. He remembers when He raised Jesus from the dead.

Christ was free from our sin and our sickness. Both had been put away before His Resurrection.

The Word declares that "By His stripes we were healed."

The whole problem is our recognition of the absolute truthfulness of that Word.

It is not good taste to ask Him to heal us, for He has already done it.

This truth came with a shock when I first saw it. He declared that we are healed; therefore we are.

The only problem now is to get in perfect harmony with His Word.

If He declares we are healed, then our part is to thank Him for the work He has already accomplished.

Our confession imprisons us or sets us free.

A strong confession coupled with a corresponding action on the Word brings God on the scene.

Holding fast to one's confession when the senses contradict shows that one has become established in the Word.

A Satan-inspired confession is always dangerous. Remember that he brought that disease, put it upon you.

Your acknowledgement of the disease is like signing for a package that the express company has left you. Satan then has the receipt for your disease. You have accepted it.

"Surely He hath borne our sickness and carried our disease" is God's receipt for our perfect healing.

A positive confession dominates circumstances, while a vacillating confession permits circumstances to govern one.

Your confession is what God says about your disease.

A negative confession will make the disease stronger.

Then your confession heals or keeps you sick.

The confession of your lips should have your heart's full agreement.

You Are a Faith-Man,
A Faith-Woman

You can be bold in your Christian life through knowing you are a faith-man, a faith-woman. What a blessing to know for sure that, no matter how you may feel, God says that faith is something you already have. It is a gift from Him!

Never call yourself a doubting Thomas. It was not the doubts of Thomas that honoured the Lord. It was the faith of those who took Him at His Word that brought His commendation and divine response. If you talk of being a doubting Thomas, then you close the door to the provisions God has for you in Christ. "For therein is the righteousness of God revealed from faith to faith; as it is written, The just shall live by faith" Romans 1:17.

"For you are all the children of God by faith in Christ Jesus" Galatians 3:26. Never chide yourself that you don't have faith. That is totally unscriptural because it's by faith that you became God's child. "For by grace are you saved through faith, and that not of yourselves, it is the gift of God" Ephesians 2:8.

"God has dealt to every man the measure of faith" Romans 12:3. There is no disputing this fact: God has given you the measure of faith. Notice, not just **a** measure, but **the** measure. It matters not how small your faith is, quantity of faith is not what is important with Jesus. He declared that faith even as a grain of mustard seed can move a mountain!

Not only do you have the measure of faith, but you have the spirit of faith. "We, having the same spirit of faith, according as it is written, I believe and therefore have I spoken, we also believe and therefore speak" II Corinthians 4:13. This spirit of faith you have is expressed by believing in your heart and speaking with your mouth.

"Be not slothful, but followers of them who, through faith and patience, inherit the promises" Hebrews 6:12. Faith is not a magic button you press to obtain what you need from God instantly. Patience is coupled with faith in inheriting the promises of God for your life.

God's title for us in the Bible is believers, never doubters. It's natural for us to function in faith because that's the nature of our lives: faith people. In fact, God says His household is one of faith. "As we have therefore opportunity, let us do good unto all men, especially unto them who are of the household of faith" Galatians 6:10.

Confess these words boldly, "I am a faith-man, a faith-woman. Faith is something that I have. God has given me the measure of faith, the spirit of faith, the Word of faith is nigh me even in my mouth and in my heart" (Romans 10:8). "This is the victory that overcomes the world, even our faith" I John 5:4.

These are personal affirmations of faith in the Word:

Have Your Own Faith Life

I am not a spiritual hitchhiker, one who depends on other's faith in times of need. I have my own faith-life, just as I have my own shoes. When a crisis comes, I do not need to seek for someone else to pray the "prayer of faith" for me; I do my own praying. If sickness strikes, I am ready to be used of God to minister healing in Jesus' Name.

Romans 12:3, "God hath given to every man the measure of faith." I declare this fact: God has given me the measure of faith. God does not classify me as a doubter, an unbeliever. I am a member of the household of faith. I am a faith-man, a faith-woman. I say it often,

"Faith is something that I have, for God has given to every Christian the measure of faith."

Matthew 7:7: "Everyone that asketh receiveth." This is the word of Jesus on the subject. Jesus clearly taught that everyone should do his own asking; everyone should do his own receiving.

Acts 10:34, "I perceive that God is no respector of persons." There are no pets of divinity. God is no respector of persons. The Father has no favourites. There are no lucky people with the Lord. I am just as dear to the Father as any evangelist, pastor, missionary or teacher. I have just as much righteousness as any other Christian has, for my righteousness is based on what Jesus has done in my stead (II Corinthians 5:21).

Romans 12:12, "Continuing instant in prayer." As a result of having my own faith-life, I know that I have instant access to God. I do not have to look here or there for someone to pray, I am bold in doing my own praying. "Whatsoever ye shall ask the Father in My Name, He will give it to you" John 16:23. I have the right to pray in the Name of Jesus to my Father, just as much right as anyone else.

I am taking my place in the believer's authority. I have ceased being a spiritual hitchhiker. I can contact the Father in the Name of Jesus as well as anyone can. The Father loves me as much as any of His children. I am bold in my faith. I pray and expect mighty answers. I tell others that I am praying for them. Courageously, I am God's channel of blessing to minister healing and help to those in need. I fearlessly cast out demons in Jesus' Name. I dare to speak the Word confidently against all sorts of oppressions. I possess faith in the life-giving Word on my lips.

I have faith in my own faith. It is the faith of God. I have faith in my God.

Fire Words

"His Word was in mine heart as a burning fire shut up in my bones" Jeremiah 20:9.

I have experienced what Jeremiah did: His Word in mine heart as a burning fire shut up in my bones. His Words are **fire words.**

The disciples on the Emmaus road had an encounter with Jesus Christ after which "He expounded unto them in all the scriptures the things concerning Himself" Luke 23:32. Jesus' Words yet produce that heavenly heartburn. His Words are **fire words.**

Jesus said, "It is the spirit that quickeneth; the flesh profiteth nothing: the words that I speak unto you, they are spirit and they are life" John 6:63. The Words of Jesus are indeed spirit and they are life. His Words are **fire words.**

When I confess His Word, it produces a fire in my heart. Fire is cleansing. "Wherewithal shall a young man cleanse his way? by taking heed thereto according to Thy Word" Psalm 119:9. "Thy Word have I hid in mine heart, that I might not sin against Thee" Psalm 119:11. His Words cleanse my spirit. His Words are **fire words.**

My prayer in relation to the Word: "Open Thou mine eyes, that I may behold the wondrous things out of Thy law" Psalm 119:18. When the Holy Spirit opens the Word to my spirit, that Word creates a fire within my bosom. His Words are **fire words.**

"So mightily grew the Word of God and prevailed" Acts 19:20. The Word has prevailing power: power to save, power to heal, power to quicken, power to create, power to subdue all foes. His Words are **fire words.**

The Two Confessions

Our faith is measured by our confession. Our usefulness in the Lord's work is measured by our confession.

Sooner or later we become what we confess.

There is the confession of our heart, and the confession of our lips.

When the confession of our lips perfectly harmonizes with the confession of our hearts, and these two confessions confirm God's Word, then we become mighty in our prayer life.

Many people have a negative confession.

They are always telling what they are not, telling of their weakness, of their failings, of their lack of money, their lack of ability, and their lack of health.

Invariably they go to the level of their confession.

A spiritual law that few of us have recognized is that our confessions rule us.

When we confess His Lordship and our hearts fully agree, then we turn our lives over into His care.

That is the end to worry, the end of fear, the beginning of faith.

When we believe that He arose from the dead for us, and that by His Resurrection He conquered the adversary and put him to nought for us, when this becomes the confession of our lips and our hearts, we become a power for God.

If we have accepted Him as our Saviour and confessed Him as our Lord, we are New Creations; we have Eternal Life; we have the position of sons; we are heirs of God and joint heirs with Jesus Christ.

The moment that we recognize the fact of His actual Resurrection, then we know that the sin problem is settled; we know that Satan has been eternally defeated for us.

We know that we are in union with Deity.

We know that we have come into the family of God.

We know that the ability of God has become ours.

This may not dawn on us all at once, but as we study the Word and act upon it, live in it, and let it live in us, it becomes slowly perhaps, but surely a living reality.

That reality is developed through our confession.

We confess His Lordship and we declare before the world that He is our Shepherd and that we do not want.

We confess that He makes us to lie down in green pastures, and that He leads us beside the waters of stillness.

We confess that He has restored our souls to a sweet, wonderful fellowship with Him.

We confess that He has made us New Creations, that old things have passed away and behold all things have become new, and that we have become the Righteousness of God in Christ.

We confess fearlessly before the world our utter oneness and union with Him.

We declare that He is the Vine and we are the branches; that the branches and the Vine are one.

We declare that we are partakers of the Divine Nature that dwelt in Him as He walked in Galilee.

These are our confessions.

We have come to know that Satan is defeated, that demons are subject to the Name of Jesus in our lips, that disease cannot exist in the presence of the Living Christ in us.

Now we dare to act on what we know the Word teaches.

We dare to take our place and confess before the world that what the Word says about us is true.

We are done with the confession of failure, of weakness, of inability, because God has become our ability, God has become our sufficiency and He has made us sufficient as ministers of a New Covenant.

We confess that He has taken us out of the old realm where failure reigned, into the new realm of victory, joy, and peace.

As we make our confession and act on the Word, our faith grows and our Redemption becomes a reality.

THE RIGHT CONFESSION

Jesus said, "For I spake not from myself; but the Father that sent me, he hath given me a commandment, what I should speak" John 12:49.

Every healing that Jesus performed was wrought through His Father's Word. Every Word that He spoke was the Father's Word.

Jesus knew who He was; He knew His place; He knew His work.

He was always positive in His message. He knew the words that He spoke were His Father's Words.

He took His place as a Son. He acted His part.

He continually confessed His Sonship.

Jesus always confessed what He was.

He said, "I am the Good Shepherd. I am the Bread of Life. I am the Water of Life. God is My Father. I am the Light of the Word."

In John 5:19-30 Jesus makes ten statements about Himself.

They are really confessions, and every one of them links Him up with Deity.

He was speaking His Father's own Word.

John 7:29 "I know Him; because I am from Him, and He sent me."

He not only confessed what He was, but He also fearlessly confessed what man would be after he became a New Creation.

John 15:5 "I am the vine, ye are the branches."

John 7:38-39 "He that believeth on me, as the scripture hath said, from within him shall flow rivers of living water. But this spake he of the Spirit, which they that believed on him were to receive: for the Spirit was not yet given; because Jesus was not yet glorified."

What a confession that was and how real it became on the Day of Pentecost!

John 8:54 "If I glorify myself, my glory is nothing: it is my Father that glorifieth me; of whom ye say, that he is your God; and ye have not known him: but I know Him; and if I should say, I know him not, I shall be like unto you, a liar: but I know him, and keep his word."

John 17:5 "And now Father, glorify thou me with thine own self with the glory which I had with thee before the world was."

That was a remarkable testimony.

John 17:26 "And I made known unto them thy name, and will make it known."

Jesus knew the new name that God was to receive.

John 17:6 "I manifested thy name unto the men whom thou gavest me out of the world."

I have a conviction that the new name which Jesus speaks of here is "Father."

No one had ever called Him "Father" before.

John 9:35-36 "Jesus heard that they had cast him out; and finding him, he said, Dost thou believe on the Son of God?

He answered and said, And who is he, Lord, that I may believe on him?"

Jesus then confessed who He really was.

In the 37th verse Jesus said to the man who had been blind, "Thou has both seen him, and he it is that speaketh with thee."

Jesus openly declared that He was the Son of God.

In John 4:26 we have another startling confession.

He was talking with the woman of Samaria and He confessed that He was the Messiah, the Son of God.

Jesus Knew Who He Was
Nearly every miracle that Jesus performed

was performed with the Father's Words in Jesus' lips.

Jesus revealed the will of the Father.

John 4:34, "My meat is to do the will of him that sent me, and to accomplish his work."

John 5:30 "I seek not mine own will, but the will of him that sent me."

John 6:38 "I am come down from heaven, not to do mine own will, but the will of him that sent me."

John 8:29 "For I do always the things that are pleasing to him."

What a picture of the Master! He had no personal ambitions, no personal ends to achieve. He was simply doing the will of His Father, unveiling the Father until He could say, "He that hath seen me hath seen the Father" (John 14:9).

The less worldly ambitions we have, the less worldly desires, the more fully the Father will unveil Himself to us.

His Words in our lips will perform the same prodigies that His Words performed in Jesus' lips.

Self-seeking limits one.

The selfish man is a limited man.

He who lives in the Word and lets the Word live in him, he who practices the Word and acts upon it, is the one who reveals the Father.

When we act upon the Word of God we unveil the Father.

Review These Facts

Few of us realize that our confession imprisons us. The right kind of confession will set us free.

It is not only our thinking; it is our words, our conversation, that builds power or weakness into us.

Our words are the coins in the Kingdom of Faith. Our words snare us and hold us in captivity, or they set us free and become powerful in the lives of others.

It is what we confess with our lips that really dominates our inner being.

We unconsciously confess what we believe.

If we talk sickness, it is because we believe in sickness. If we talk weakness and failure, it is because we believe in weakness and failure.

It is surprising what faith people have in wrong things.

They firmly believe in cancer, ulcers of the stomach, tuberculosis, and other incurable diseases. Their faith in that disease rises to the point where it utterly dominates them, rules them. They become its absolute slaves.

They get the habit of confessing their weakness and their confession adds to the strength of their weakness. They confess their lack of faith and they are filled with doubts.

They confess their fear and they become more fearful. They confess their fear of disease and the disease grows under the confession.

They confess their lack and they build up a sense of lack which gains the supremacy in their lives.

When we realize that we will never rise above our confession, we are getting to the place where God can really begin to use us.

You confess that by His stripes you are healed; hold fast to your confession and no disease can stand before you.

Whether we realize it or not, we are sowing words just as Jesus said in Luke 8:11, "The seed is the Word of God." The sower went forth to sow and the seed he was sowing was the Word of God.

That is the seed we should sow. Others are sowing Sense Knowledge seeds of fear and doubt.

It is when we confess the Word of God, declare with emphasis that "By His stripes I am healed" or "My God supplies every need of mine" and hold fast to our confession that we see our deliverance.

Our words beget faith or doubt in others.

Revelation 12:11 declares "And they overcame him because of the blood of the Lamb, and because of the word of their testimony."

They overcame him with the Word of God that was in their testimony. They conquered the devil with words.

Most of the sick that Jesus healed during His ministry were healed with words.

God created the Universe with words: faith-filled words.

Jesus said, "Thy faith has made thee whole."

He said to dead Lazarus, "Come forth." His words raised the dead.

Satan is overcome by words, he is whipped by words.

Our lips become the means of transportation of God's deliverance from heaven to man's need here on earth.

We use God's Word. We whisper, "In Jesus' Name, demon, come out of him."

Jesus said, "In my Name ye shall cast out demons, in my Name ye shall lay hands on the sick and they shall recover."

All with words!

I question whether the hands do more than to register to the senses. It is the Word that heals.

Jesus said, "Whatsoever ye demand in my Name that will I do." (In the Greek the word *ask* is *demand.*)

We are demanding just as Peter did at the Beautiful Gate when he said, "In the name of Jesus Christ of Nazareth, walk."

Words healed that man.

Now we make our confession of words. We hold fast to our confession. We refuse to be defeated in our confession.

John 8:32, "And ye shall know the truth, and the truth shall make you free."

Or John 8:36 "If therefore the Son shall make you free, ye shall be free indeed."

We know that the Son has set us free and we confess it.

Jesus is the High Priest of our confession.

Christ conquered the enemies of humanity: Satan, sin, sickness, fear, death and want.

He made them captives and He set them free.

Hebrews 4:14 tells us to hold fast to the confession of our faith.

"Having then a great high priest, who hath passed through the heavens, Jesus the Son of God, let us hold fast our confession."

That confession is faith speaking. It is our victory over the enemy. It is our confidence.

Colossians 2:5 in one of our translations reads, "For although, as you say, I am absent from the body, yet in spirit am I present with you and am delighted to witness your good discipline and the solid front presented by your faith in Christ."

That "solid front" means continual confession of victory.

We never confess anything but victory.

Romans 8:37 "Nay, in all these things we are more than conquerors through him that loved us."

Jesus disarmed the principalities and powers which fought against Him and put them to an open shame. (This is Colossians 2:15 from Connybeare's Translation.)

We should stop making the wrong kind of confession, and begin at once to learn HOW to confess and WHAT to confess.

We should begin to confess that we are what He says we are, and hold fast to that confession in the face of every contrary evidence.

We refuse to be weak or to acknowledge weakness.

We refuse to have anything to do with a wrong confession.

We are what He says we are.

We hold fast to that confession with a fearless consciousness that God's Word can never fail.

I Am Sick and Tired of Being Sick and Tired

"And ought not this woman, being a daughter of Abraham, whom Satan has bound, lo these eighteen years, be loosed from this bond on the Sabbath day?" Luke 13:16.

I rebel in Jesus' Name against the bonds of the devil. The Bible does not call my sickness a blessing. The Bible calls my sickness a bondage. Sickness is a bond of the devil and from every bond I "ought to be loosed."

I am sick and tired of being sick and tired because I have every right to be healed. It cost my Lord dearly to take upon Himself my infirmities and sicknesses. I rebel against sickness with these words, "Get thee behind me, devil, for thus it is written, Himself took our infirmities and bare our sicknesses" Matthew 8:17.

I have every right to be healed because of the substitutionary sacrifice of Christ Himself. The only reason worthy of basing my faith for healing is what Jesus has provided for me. His blood alone qualifies me for healing. My right to receive from God is based on the blood. I rebel against Satan's trespassing of God's property by this declaration, "Satan, get thee hence. For thus it is written, I was made nigh to God by the blood of Christ" Ephesians 2:13.

I rebel against this **rebel the devil,** because I have a right to be healed, not because of how good or sincere I have been, but because of those bleeding stripes. I rebel by these words, "Devil, be thou gone, for thus it is written, with His stripes we are healed" Isaiah 53:5.

I am not ignorant of Satan's devices and I have learned by the Holy Spirit to discern his work of oppression against me. I'm sick and tired of being sick and tired, so I overcome his works by the blood of Jesus and the Word in my testimony. I rebel against this thief by these words, "Devil, I resist you in Jesus' Name for I am depending entirely on the merits of Christ Jesus, by whose stripes I was healed" (I Peter 2:24).

I shall stand my ground fearlessly in receiving my healing in the Name of Jesus. Never again will I be the devil's "dumping ground" of his foul spirits of oppression. I rebel by this statement of authority, "Devil, the blood of Jesus defeats you and I resist you because it is written, the anointing shall destroy the yoke" (Isaiah 10:27).

BY HIS STRIPES I AM HEALED

"With His stripes we are healed" Isaiah 53:5. This prophecy given to Isaiah was concerning our Lord Jesus Christ and the bleeding wounds He was to endure to provide for His people. It is a finished work. Jesus has endured the striping.

No matter what symptoms are present, by His stripes I am healed. I confess this fact in the presence of symptoms that would contradict. "We walk by faith, and not by sight" II Corinthians 5:7.

Regardless of other opinions about my health, by His stripes I am healed. Others may think I look badly, they may pass their opinion about my state of health, but the truth prevails: by His stripes I am healed.

In spite of past experiences, by His stripes I am healed. I may have sought for healing before that was not manifested, but this is a new day for me: by His stripes I am healed.

When pain strikes my body, by His stripes I am healed. It may be true that pain is there in my body, but I know greater truth: by His stripes I am healed!

When things appear all wrong in health condition, His truth still prevails, by His stripes I am healed. When things appear all right and my health examinations are solid, it's because by His stripes I am healed.

Wherever I am, regardless how I feel, I hold fast my joyful confession of His truth, by His stripes I am healed.

"Who His own self bare our sins in His own body on the tree, that we, being dead to sins, should live unto righteousness; by whose stripes you were healed" I Peter 2:24.

I AM STRONG

"Let the weak say, I am strong" Joel 3:10.

I am strong! This is the paradox of faith: to say I am strong when I am weak. This is faith's confession: I am strong.

No matter what I think of myself, I am strong. Regardless of other's opinions about my life, I am strong. When I feel the weakest, I am strong.

In spite of past experiences of succumbing to weakness, I rise up with a new testimony of faith: I am strong. It is not just when I feel strong that I say I am strong. But it is when I even feel weak that I declare, I am strong.

God commands me to say, I am strong. This is saying what God says about my life. This is the language of faith. This is the language of victory.

Who am I? I am strong. Whatever else I may be, I am strong. Wherever I am, I am strong.

What I confess I possess. What I say is what I get. I confess, "I am strong," and I possess strength.

Why can I be so sure? Not only in Joel 3:10 but in countless other scriptures, God declares that He is my strength. So I gladly obey His command and say it, "I am strong." Never do I say, "I am weak." This would be disobedience to my God, it would grieve the Holy Spirit.

"Let the weak say, I am strong" Joel 3:10.

WHAT AM I FEARING?

Am I afraid of untimely death? Am I afraid of a heart attack? Is my fear of cancer? Do I have a fear of some calamity? Do I fear the loss of the affection of my loved ones? Do I have a dreaded fear of flying in an airplane? Is the fear of man prevelant in my life?

If there is any fear in my heart, I must be freed from it. Fear is an actual spirit that moves from without to take up occupancy within my life. Satan takes advantage of my giving place to fear and sees that the thing which I fear is reproduced in my life.

"For the thing which I greatly feared is come upon me and that which I was afraid of is come unto me" Job 3:25. When Job made this confession, he was on the ash heap of great suffering with boils from the top of his head to the soles of his feet. He had lost his family, his earthly possessions. Job evidently had entertained this fear for a long time by his admission that "the thing which I greatly feared has come upon me and that which I was afraid of has come unto me."

What am I fearing? I must expel every spirit of fear from my life or else that negative, tormenting fear can reproduce into my life the very thing which I fear.

The Bible description of fear is not pleasant. It describes fear as tormenting, soul-snaring, the spirit of bondage, and able to reproduce itself in misery.

Luke 1:74-75 tells us a purpose of Christ's coming to this world is, "We, being delivered out of the hand of our enemies, might serve Him without fear . . . all the days of our life." That means every day we ought to be free from fear. In the Bible there is a verse against fear for every day of the year.

Now, in the Name of Jesus, I take bold action, "You satanic spirit of fear that has oppressed and vexed my life, I command you in Jesus' Name to depart from my life because it is written, God has not given us the spirit of fear, but of power, love and a sound mind" II Timothy 1:7.

The Power of Our Words

I remember that Jesus said, "Thy faith has made thee whole."

It was the faith of the person that made them whole. Then I saw that it is our words that heal us.

When we say "By His stripes I am healed" that confession brings my deliverance from the disease.

You notice he said in Romans 10:9, "That if thou shalt confess with thy mouth Jesus as Lord and believe in thy heart that God raised Him from the dead, thou shalt be saved."

Saved here means healed. It is your mouth that makes the confession. It is the confession of the faith that you have in your heart or in your spirit.

You have come to believe or to know that the word of God is absolute. He watches over every word to perform it. "No Word from God is void of power" or ability.

What does the Word of God do? The Word of God saves you. The Word of God heals you. The Word of God supplies us with finances. It is the Word that does it.

Psalm 107:20, "He sent His Word and healed us."

Jesus is that Word.

His Words were Himself.

Now I made the Word of God my Word and that Word dwells in me richly. When I speak it is the Word in my lips and I say "By His stripes I am healed."

That Word is my Word and His Word.

The moment I say it, that healing is mine.

Your words are your confession. They confirm or deny the Word of God. One of the unhappy things is that one minute we confess that we are healed. The pain comes back and we confess that we are not healed. We deny our first confession. In denying it we deny the Word that declares that we are healed.

To maintain your confession and hold fast to your confession is the secret of success and victory in the divine life.

You hold fast your confession that God laid upon Jesus your sin and that gives you eternal life.

You hold fast to your confession that by His stripes you are healed, and that gives you your healing.

You hold fast to your confession that "Nay, in all these things, ye are more than conquerors," and you are a conqueror.

You hold fast to your confession that "My God shall supply every need of yours," and every need is supplied.

You waver in your confession, and deny your confession, and you annul the Word as far as you are concerned.

Now you can see that your faith is measured by your words, or your confession.

Your confession is your estimation of the value of the Word of God.

The words that Jesus spoke are still green and fresh, giving hope and joy and victory to the multitudes.

The record of the things that He did still thrills us.

The words of the Apostle Paul are to us at times like a flame that burns; another time, the healing ointment that quiets the wound and brings the heart into fellowship with Heaven.

"The words that I speak unto you, they are spirit and life," said the Master.

Now I want you to see the effect of your words upon yourself.

Your words bring discouragement and defeat into your own life. I ask, "How are you getting along?"

You answer, "Everything has just gone wrong. The bottom seems to have fallen out of everything. I've lost my grip. I can't seem to put over anything."

That is a confession. What are its reactions on you?

You are instantly filled with self-pity and the sense of defeat.

You are robbed of the power of initiative, the ability to pick up the scattered ends and bring them together again into victory.

You can't seem to do it. Why?

Your confession has unnerved you and wrecked you.

The same thing is true when you have trouble with your husband, or someone else, and you tell that over and over again.

Every time you do, you cry and go through the deepest agony.

Had you not told it, you would have been much stronger.

Your words are poison to your own system. Your words are sometimes deadly.

When you say, "I don't believe I'll ever get over this," that is taking poison.

There is no antidote for it except the breaking of the power of that kind of confession, and beginning to speak the right kind of words and give the right kind of a confession.

You think and talk failure and you will go

down to its level.

Your words create an atmosphere that injure and break you.

There are three classes of words: neutral, colorless, empty, soulless words. These are the general conversation of most people.

They are just empty words, colorless words, words of the monotone.

You hear a preacher preaching in a monotone; there is no color, no soul, no power, or life in his words—just sounds thrown out on the air.

The second class of words is constructive words, strength-building, healing words, words of inspiration, thrilling, mighty, dominant words, words pregnant with hope, love, and victory.

Then the third class is destructive words, words filled with hatred, scandal, bitterness, jealousy, deadly virus, coming from a heart full of bitterness, sent out to wound, blight, curse, and damn.

What a tremendous place words hold.

You see what you can do with words, how you can change lives, how you can bless and build, and encourage, and lead men to master achievements.

30
DG

"How Forcible Are Right Words"

"How forcible are right words! but what doth your arguing reprove?" Job 6:25.

There is a great power in your mouth to speak right words that are forcible and dynamic in their working. Speak in the Name of Jesus. "Whatsoever ye do in *word* or deed, do all in the Name of the Lord Jesus, giving thanks to God and the Father by Him" Colossians 3:17. It's not superstition nor mysticism to speak often His wonderful Name. "The Name of the Lord is a strong tower; the righteous runneth into it and is safe" Proverbs 18:10.

Jesus gave us the right to speak in His Name. The "ask" of John 14:13-14 implies "commanding in the Name of Jesus" diseases, demons, and adverse circumstances to depart! The "ask" of John 15:16 and 16:23-24 refers to praying to the Father in the all-powerful Name of Jesus. Jesus is the Name above all names (Philippians 2:9-11). How forcible is His majestic Name! I challenge you to speak His Name often. Right now say "Jesus" three times!

In crusades in Nagercoil, Tamul Nadu, and Trivandrum, Kerala, India, I faced thousands of people each night in our open air crusades. Over and over I invoked the Name of Jesus in commanding the diseases to depart. In Nagercoil, 77 notable miracles were recorded. Similar results took place in Trivandrum. You too, can receive healing through His Name. "And His Name through faith in His Name hath made this man strong, whom ye see and know: yea, the faith which is by Him hath given him this perfect soundness in the presence of you all" Acts 3:16.

In India I had the immense joy of leading tens of thousands of people to saving faith in Jesus Christ. As these multitudes believed in the death, burial, and the resurrection of Jesus Christ and confessed Him as Lord of their lives, they received Everlasting life! You, too, can be saved now. "For the same Lord over all is rich unto all that call upon Him. For whosoever shall call upon the Name of the Lord shall be saved" Romans 10:12-13.

Words of praise are forcible words. Praise is the spark-plug of faith, the one thing needed to get your faith airborne, enabling you to soar above deadly doubt. Speak words of praise often.

The Value of a Positive Confession

You remember in II Corinthians 1:17, "Dare you say that, when I make arrangements, I make them like shifty men of the world, with the intention of changing 'I will' into 'I will not' if it suits me? By all the faithfulness of God I swear it, my utterances to you never waver between Yes and No—just as in the proclamation in your midst of God's son, Jesus, as the Messiah by Himself, by Sylvanus, and by Timotheus, there was never any wavering between affirmation and negation—no? by the inspiration of God it was ever one consistent affirmative. The same is true of all the promises of God; they are affirmed by His 'I will,' ay, and they are sealed by His 'Amen'; and so God is glorified through our faith in his promises." (Way's trans).

"For Jesus Christ, Son of God, who was proclaimed among you by us, that is, by Sylvanus and Timothy and me, was not wavering between 'Yes' and 'No' but in him is the everlasting 'Yes.' (Montgomery's trans).

Many spoil their confession by wavering between the positive "yes" and the faltering "no." When the heart can say "yes," a ringing positive "yes" to the Word, then reality begins to assert itself in their confession. It must begin in the heart. The heart must begin to say "Yes" to the Word of God.

You are sick. You are bold in your confession of your sickness, and you are faltering in your confession that by His stripes you are healed.

You can't have two confessions. One is going to destroy the other. If your confession of sickness is stronger than your confession of the Word, then the sickness gains the ascendancy and you live in defeat.

If your financial need is great and your confession is one of continual need, the Scripture, "My God shall supply every need of yours," is made of no effect. By your wrong confession, faith is destroyed.

When will we learn to have an eternal "yes" toward the Word? A positive, clear-cut confession? If God says that it is then it is. If God says that I am, I am. If He says "Greater is he that is in you than he that is in the world," then I am master.

If He declares that I am the righteousness

of God in Christ, then I am. If he whispers "Nay in all these things you are more than a conqueror," I say "Amen." So God has my Amen to everyone of these scriptures.

If He whispers "I can do all things in him who is my ability and strength" I whisper "Amen."

I align my confession with everyone of his declarative statements in regard to myself in Christ.

He says, "Surely he hath borne my sicknesses and carried my diseases, and I have come to esteem him as the one who was stricken, smitten of God and afflicted. He was wounded for iniquities; the chastisement of my peace was upon him; and with His stripes I am healed," and I say "Amen."

I have no disease then and I maintain my confession before the world.

Didn't He say He put them on Jesus? Yes. Didn't Jesus put them away? Yes. Then I am not going to claim them as mine. They are not mine. They belong to an enemy that dumped them on me, but I refuse to be his dumping ground any longer, and so I say "in the Name of Jesus, Satan, come and get your old diseases. I refuse to own them, to have aught to do with them," and he comes and gets them. He has to do it because he must yield to the authority of the Name.

He can't hold me in poverty. He can't make want my master. No, the one who turned water into wine, who fed the multitude with five loaves and two little fishes is my Lord and my Master. He is my bread provider.

He is my strength.

He is all that I need.

I rest in Him. I walk in Him.

His ability has become my ability and His grace is my grace.

I bathe in His love.

I bask in His light.

I revel in His wisdom.

I am His and He is mine.

"The Lord Is the Strength of My Life"

These are great confessions; affirm them with confidence.

I. The Lord is the strength of my *mind*, so today I think sound, healthy thoughts. I think upon those things that are true, honest, just, pure, lovely and of a good report. A strong mind is a positive mind, the mind of Christ. "I have the mind of Christ" I Corinthians 2:16.

II. The Lord is the strength of my *ears*, so I hear well today. Seven times in Revelation 2 and 3 the command comes, "He that hath an ear, let him hear what the Spirit saith . . ." Most important, with my renewed, sound, strong mind, I hear what the Spirit saith unto me.

III. The Lord is the strength of my *eyes*, so I have good vision for today. I see others through eyes of love, kindness, and good will.

IV. The Lord is the strength of my *mouth*,

so I speak those words that are edifying, ministering grace to those who hear me. Isaiah 50:4, "The Lord God hath given me the tongue of the learned, that I should know how to speak a word in season to him that is weary: he wakeneth morning by morning, he wakeneth mine ear to hear as the learned." I refrain from speaking those words that are negative, destructive, corrupt, critical, harsh or unkind.

V. The Lord is the strength of my *heart*, so I have a good sound heartbeat for today. My prayer, "Lord be thou the strength of my physical heart as long as I serve you on this earth. Yea, 70 years and by reason of strength 80 years or more." Oh heart, do your good work for this day.

VI. The Lord is the strength of my *hands*, so that whatsoever my hands find to do, they do it with all their might.

VII. The Lord is the strength of every *organ, tissue, bone, fiber, nerve* and *cell* in my body. The Lord is the strength of my life from the top of my head to the soles of my feet. When my feet become tired, sore, aching, the Lord renews my feet by the invigoration of His strength.

VIII. The Lord is the strength of my *life*— my whole life—spirit, soul and body. He infuses strength into the hidden man of the heart.

IX. My affirmations for today: Daniel 11:32,

"The people that know their God shall be strong and do exploits." Psalm 29:11, "The Lord will give *strength* unto His people; the Lord will bless His people with peace." Philippians 4:13, "I can do all things through Christ which strengtheneth me" (not weakeneth me). Nehemiah 8:10, "The joy of the Lord is my strength." Deuteronomy 33:25, "As my days are, so shall my strength be." II Corinthians 12:10, "When I am weak, then am I strong."

X. I affirm it five times:

"The Lord is the strength of my life"

"The Lord is the strength of my life"

"The Lord is the strength of my life"

"The Lord is the strength of my life"

"The Lord is the strength of my life"

XI. I think strength. I believe in the Lord's strength. I talk strength. Joel 3:10, "Let the weak say, I am strong." I confess I am strong. Often I say, "Strength, Strength, Strength," as I speak the Word to my spirit. Praise the Lord!

XII. I, _____, affirm the Lord is the strength of my life.

33
EWK

By His Stripes I Am Healed

This is Faith's Testimony against the Testimony of the Senses and Reason.

Reason says, "The pain is still there."

The Senses make Reason's Testimony a duet.

Faith refuses to acknowledge feeling or sight of the eyes.

It stands squarely upon what God has spoken.

His Word says, "Surely He has borne our sickness," and if God says that He bore our sickness, it is true, for that Word is a part of God, and every Word that God has spoken is a part of Himself.

We can say confidently that what God says IS.

The same Scripture declares that, "By His stripes we are healed."

That was spoken seven hundred years before our diseases were laid upon Christ.

It is now two-thousand years since that was fulfilled on Calvary.

Our diseases and sicknesses, our sins and infirmities were all borne by the Master: so, if He bore them, it is wrong for us to bear them—because by our bearing them we nullify what He did!

We stand squarely upon the Living Word of God.

We refuse to listen to any other voice.

Mark 16:18, "They shall lay hands on the sick, and they shall recover."

Then, when I lay hands on the sick, God says they shall recover!

This Word is Authoritative as any that ever fell from the lips of the Master.

Faith declares that it is done.

The moment that our hands are laid upon that sick one, Faith says, "Thank Thee Father, I am Healed."

By His stripes I am set free from that old disease.

Faith always speaks before God acts.

Faith's speaking causes God's action.

Faith says, "God has declared I am Healed, and whatever God declares, IS."

When God said, "Let there be lights in the firmament of Heaven" the lights became and when God says, "By His stripes you are healed," it becomes a fact because no Word from God is void of power.

Romans 8:11, "But if the Spirit of Him that raised up Jesus from the dead shall quicken also your mortal bodies through His Spirit that dwelleth in you."

This is God talking about our bodies, that are to respond to His Word.

These bodies are His home, the place where He is enthroned and reigns as a King.

This Living God who has said, "By His stripes ye are healed," is here in our bodies to make good that Living Word.

34
DG

Have Rugged Faith

Have you ever noticed that the people who constantly talk about sickness have a large portion of it? Did you ever observe that those who are talking about fear constantly are usually quite fearful? If you think it through, you will discover that the ones who constantly talk about lack, experience lack as their master. It's a Bible fact that our words produce the kind of life we have. What you confess you posess. What you say is what you get. Jesus said, "Out of the abundance of the heart the mouth speaketh."

There is a verse in Job that has intrigued me a great deal. It also represents the power of words. It is a further Bible proof that what you say is what you get. This passage reads like this: "Thou shalt also decree a thing, and it shall be established unto thee" Job 22:28. By your words you decree things, and God says, "It shall be established unto thee." It shall become a part of your life. Confessing or decreeing a thing is a verbal exercise that brings a response: *It shall be established unto thee.*

This is in harmony with what Jesus said in Mark 11:23, "Whosoever shall say . . . and doubt not in his heart, but shall believe that those things which he saith shall come to pass, he shall have whatsoever he saith." Whatever you say, or decree, will become reality in your life. The Bible says so.

There are many other Bible evidences that verify that what you continually speak is what you will have. I trust you will allow these statements of the Bible to sink deeply into your life, that when you decree things, you will have those things established in your life. Who says so? God says so and what God says is right, absolutely right. And God says that when you or I decree a thing, it shall be established unto us. Jesus said it, "He shall have whatsoever he saith."

These verses, among others, should serve as a challenge to us to be sure to speak words that harmonize with God's Word. We must bring our testimony up to the level of the Holy scriptures, to train our lips to speak only that which is in line with "thus saith the Lord."

The Lord gave me a beautiful healing of

a growth on the side of my head that was scheduled for surgery. I dared to decree, "by His stripes I am healed." After I decreed that, it was established unto me and surely enough by miraculous intervention, the growth disappeared.

For several years I owed a Saskatchewan radio station several thousand dollars. It seemed it was almost impossible to have the money to pay the debt. I began to affirm, "I decree that my God shall supply all the money to pay the Saskatchewan radio station." God who watches over His word to perform it honored my decree, and it became an established fact. On December 31, 1977, I paid off the last $850 of that account, praise the Lord!

THE DEVIL HEARS ALSO

Please don't forget this fact: the devil hears your testimony too. The Bible says we overcome the devil by the Word of God in our testimony (Revelation 12:11). But if we have a testimony that lacks the Word of God in it, then the devil will easily rout us. Or if our testimony is not in harmony with God's Word, then the adversary will usurp an advantage.

If your testimony is one of sickness, then that develops the sickness stronger in your body. In the face of sickness, let your testimony courageously be that of God's own Word. Say Matthew 8:17, "Jesus Himself took my infirmities and bare my sickness."

Talk about God's Word. Talk about God's goodness to you. Fill your lips with praise for answers to prayers that you have asked. As you do so, your faith will grow by leaps and bounds.

On the contrary, if you talk about your trials, your testings, your difficulties, your lack of faith, then your faith will shrivel. It will lose its vitality in your life.

The Bible commands in Hebrews 10:23, "Let us hold fast our confession of faith, for He is faithful that promised." Our part in this life of faith is to hold fast our confession; God's part is to fulfill faithfully His Word to us.

I have found that in my years of walking the faith walk, the victories have been mine as I have tenaciously held fast to God's Word. If I departed from God's Word to my feelings or appearances, then I was defeated.

For instance, when my family and I were hopelessly stuck in Tel Aviv, Israel, it seemed that our plans for extensive ministry in Africa were stymied. Every sensual evidence was arrayed against us. I "heard" the airline agents say we would not get to Africa for many days. I "saw" all the other passengers leave—with my family and I standing sadly behind. I "felt" the pangs of despair at 2:00 a.m. in the morning. I knew I must not depart from God's Word to my feelings or appearances, for I would be thoroughly whipped. As I held my heart steady confessing God's Word, that supernatural Word prevailed over our dismal circumstances and within hours we were on the way to Africa.

Now the hardest battles in which you'll ever engage are along this line. But the greatest victories you'll ever win will be those when everything cries out "impossible." I do not know everything about theology, about the coming of the Lord, and all future events. But this is something I really know by beautiful experience in living the Word: when you dare to hold fast your confession of God's Word, impossibilities become realities.

I challenge you; never give in to the adversary. You and God are masters of the situation. Always remember that Jesus met defeat and conquered it. You are facing defeat everywhere but you face defeat as a master in Jesus' Name and in that Name you conquer. Don't let down. Keep up your solid front. God is for you and you can't be conquered.

When you state a thing, you actually decree that into your life. If you decree lack, you'll have lack as your master. But if you decree that God supplies your needs, you'll know His supply. If you decree weakness, then you'll have weakness. But if you decree the fact that the Lord is the strength of your life, then you will know His strength. If you decree fear, then you'll have your portion of fearful living. If you decree God's supply of courage, then you'll be courageous, rather than fearful.

Another reason you have been so defeated in life is because you have talked the language of doubt and unbelief. You can't do that without suffering the consequences. You talk doubt and doubt will arise like a giant and bind you. You talk unbelief and you will know the torment of unbelief the rest of your days. You talk how weak your faith is, and you'll be as weak as the natural man. But since you are a new creature in Christ Jesus, you should have the vocabulary of the conqueror.

What you say is what you get. What you confess is what you possess. What you decree is what you will experience. You talk failure, and whatever you do, you will fail. I challenge you to make a bold, confident confession.

Dare to be a real Jesus person. Be a nonconformist to the world crowd. Be a Jesus man, a Jesus woman. Be filled with the love of Jesus. Be filled with enthusiasm in your work. Cast out that spirit of fear in Jesus' Name. Tackle that difficult thing today that has plagued your life.

Decree right things, the things of God's Word, and wonderful things will be established unto you. Make negative decrees, and negative adverse things will be your portion in life.

Have rugged faith, the kind of faith that wins.

Make Your Words Work for You

Words are the greatest things in the world. Words are thoughts put in garments so they can be commercially used and exchanged.

Naked thoughts cannot be seen, heard, felt nor sold; just thoughts put into words have value.

Words can be of tremendous value if they are filled with the right kind of material.

Words made Austria a part of Germany in World War II.

Words invite deeds, actions.

Words stir the world, thrilling nations, firing a people with ambition or sorrow.

God helps us to use words wisely.

The Bible is made up of words, God-filled words, love-filled words.

You and I are going out to sell and to buy and to work and we will be using words today.

Let us use them as we would use gold,

handle them as though they were diamonds, choice things.

To many people words are just as common as dirt.

Others consider them a little more valuable.

But the wise man is careful of words.

I said a sentence one day and it cost me three hundred dollars. I should not have said it.

I knew a man who said just one sentence and it cost him a life time of labor.

Words are mighty things.

By words, you are saved. By words, you are lost.

I Never Rise Above My Confession

"Let us hold fast the confession of our faith without wavering; (for He is faithful that promised)" Hebrews 10:23.

(Speak this as a personal confession of faith.)

I never rise above my confession. A negative confession will lower me to the level of that confession. It is what I confess with my lips that really controls me. My confession imprisons me if it is negative, or it sets me free if it is positive. What I say is what I get. "He shall have whatsoever he saith" Mark 11:23.

If I am always telling of my failings and my lack of faith, invariably I go to the level of this confession. When I confess lack of faith, that increases doubt. Every time I confess doubts and fears, I am confessing my faith in Satan and deny the ability and grace of God. When I confess doubt, I am inprisoned by my own words. Proverbs 6:2, "Thou art snared by the words of thy mouth."

A wrong confession shuts the Father out of my life, and lets Satan in. If I doubt His Word, it is because I believe something else that is contrary to His Word. I refuse to have anything to do with a wrong confession. When I realize I never rise above my confession, I am getting to the place where God can use me. Ephesians 4:29, "Let no corrupt communication proceed out of your mouth, but that which is good, to the use of edifying, that it may minister grace unto the hearers." A wrong confession is corrupt communication. I *speak only that which is good* to the use of edifying.

"Neither give place to the devil" Ephesians 4:27. I refuse to testify for the adversary. I *think* faith, I *speak* faith, I *act* faith. I am ruled by my confessions. What I confess with my lips is what really dominates me. I make my lips do their duty. I refuse to allow my lips destroy the effectiveness of the Word of God in my case. If I waver in my faith, I will receive nothing from the Lord. It is with my heart I believe, and with my mouth I confess unto salvation, healing, supply, deliverance, strength! I not only confess with my lips, also I do not deny in my heart. I refuse to confess with my lips, but in my heart say, "But the Word is not true in my case." The confession of my lips has no value if my heart repudiates it. I wise up with the Word and rise up to possess my possessions!

The Father's Words in Jesus' Lips

When we learn that the Father and His Word are one, the Bible will become a new book. When we realize that it is the Master speaking directly to us, then it becomes a reality.

Jesus tells us in John 12:47-48, "And if any man hear my sayings, and keep them not, I judge him not: for I come not to judge the world, but to save the world. He that rejecteth me, and receiveth not my sayings, hath one that judgeth him: the word that I spake, the same shall judge him in the last day. For I spake not from myself: but the Father that sent me, he hath given me a commandment, what I should say, and what I should speak."

Nowhere does Jesus claim to be original, that the words that he speaks are original. Always He declares that He is speaking His Father's words.

When Jesus healed the sick, it was the Word

of the Father upon His lips. When He said, "Lazarus, come forth," it was the Father's words that did the miracle.

When He spoke to the tree and it died, it was the Father's Word upon His lips. When He hushed the sea, when He multiplied the bread, when he healed the sick and raised the dead, it was the Father's Word upon His lips.

When He said, "I am the light of the world," He was but speaking what His Father gave Him to speak.

The Father's words in Jesus' lips, then, brought life to the dead, healing to the sick, perfect limbs to the maimed, food for the hungry, sight for the blind, and deliverance from the fear of a watery grave.

Can you grasp the significance of this?

Jesus did it all with words.

Now He has given to us His words. He is the surety of this New Covenant from Matthew to Revelation. We can use His words now. His words in our lips will perform the same kind of miracles that the Father's words did in His lips.

It is a problem of our utilizing what He has given to us. To illustrate, He has filled the earth with oil, but if no one paid any attention to it, and we had reached a place, we will assume, where we desperately needed oil and gas, but we have ignored the storehouse that is filled with oil, that is an example of what we are doing with His living word.

Today we have power to heal every sick one, we have ability to meet every need of men and women around us, and those needs are greater than the need for oil or gas.

We have the words that have healing, that have salvation, that have deliverance, that have joy, that have peace, that have rest. We have the words that will build faith into the discouraged, strength into the weak, hope into the heart of the hopeless, and deliverance for those who are being held in captivity.

We refrain from using the words that will do it.

You understand that God's ability is wrapped up in His words. Those words have been given to us. We can use them.

How desperately the world needs them. Now you begin to speak His words. Let them become living things in your lips. You dare to say to the sick. "In Jesus' Name you are healed," to the man in captivity, "In Jesus' Name, demon, leave this man."

Dare take your place.

Talk Your Way Forward

In 1961, I was challenged by a man, "Talk the way you would like to be and you will be the way you talk."

I began to talk. Not the way things were then, but the way I would like them to be. I discovered this harmonized with scripture, "Whosoever shall say to this mountain, be thou removed, and be thou cast into the sea, and shall not doubt in his heart, but shall believe that those things which he saith shall come to pass, he shall have whatsoever he saith" Mark 11:23.

I had just lost by repossession my home and five rooms of furniture. I had talked poverty and reaped poverty. I changed my tune and began to affirm, "GOD GIVETH ME WEALTH AND HEALTH." This harmonized with 3 John 2, "Beloved, I wish above all things thou mayest prosper and be in health, even as thy soul prospereth." To say, "God giveth me wealth and health," when I was without any money, home, or furniture, with my family living in two little rooms in a motel at Victoria, this was "talking the way I would like to be, so I would be the way I talked."

Another Power Poem I began to live by, "WHAT I CONFESS I POSSESS." I was learning that WHAT YOU SAY IS WHAT YOU GET. I began to confess, "My God shall supply all my need according to His riches in glory by Christ Jesus" Philippians 4:19. I disciplined my lips and held my heart steady unto the supply of a home, furniture, but most of all, for a ministry that would enable me to be an achiever in Jesus, a positive help to poverty-shackeled, fettered and oppressed people.

So I began to sing, "I SEE I AM FREE." I knew Jesus came to liberate the captives and I was a captive to the oppressions of fear, anxiety, worry, frustration. "Stand fast therefore in the liberty wherewith Christ has made you free, and be not entangled again with the yoke of bondage" Galatians 5:1. I learned to rebel against poverty, failure and tyranny in every form.

I talked like this: I am an achiever in life. I always do things that please my Lord. I shall utilize the modern communications methods to preach the Gospel. I shall succeed as a radio broadcaster. The Holy Spirit has put many books into my heart. I shall write those books.

I talked my way forward. I confessed the Word. I refused negative confessions.

Pertaining to the home we purchased in Surrey, I began to affirm: I shall make every payment without fail. The devil can never steal this home from us. I shall furnish it adequately for my family. We shall all be happy and fulfilled in this home.

My previous record was one of failure, one dilemma after another in financial matters. I had not succeeded as a radio broadcaster. I had no way to publish, even though my heart was burning with truths to write.

I kept on talking the way I would like to be, and praise the Lord, I became the way I talked. I was enabled by God to weather the storms and triumph through His grace.

Of course, my principal source of talking material was the Word of God. Jesus declared, "The words that I speak unto you, they are spirit and they are life" John 6:63. "The Word of God is quick and powerful and sharper than a two-edged sword" Hebrews 4:12.

This "speaking forth principle" is the very ingredient of faith. II Corinthians 4:13, "We then also having the same spirit of faith, according as it is written, I believed, therefore have I spoken; we also believe, therefore do we speak." This scripture teaches us how faith operates: believing first of all in your heart, then speaking forth what you believe. It is the WORD we believe; therefore, it is the life-giving Word that we speak.

Faith confessions have been our victory. We talked our way forward.

I confessed, "We shall be used of God to win tens of thousands to Christ." This was really in the realm of faith for in no way were we ever winning even thousands to Christ. We became the way we talked; literally tens of thousands of souls have been won to Christ.

Overcoming our pattern of failure in radio broadcasting, I began to proclaim, "We shall succeed on radio stations all over the world." That has been a glorious fact, praise the Lord.

With this intense ambition to bless the body of Christ by the faith principles I had learned through severe testings, I affirmed, "I shall be able to publish these dynamic truths of the Word to edify others." Now 20 years later, more than 20 million copies of my publications have rolled from the presses.

I testified by faith, "My five children shall grow up strong in the Lord and useful to Him." Praise God, this has been glorious reality, as they all live under the Lordship of Jesus Christ.

My confession has preceded my possession. I have confessed, "I am sold on being bold."

Through bold ministry we have witnessed supernatural results in healings and deliverances everywhere we have gone with the Good News.

What you say is what you get. What I say is what I get. I have said, "There is no room for gloom." Gloom and depression have repeatedly sought to put me into their evil grasp. I have resisted in Jesus and overcome. I might add, "A smile is my style."

We have made it our motto, "I live to give. Life is to give and not take." The giving life is the winning life.

Twenty years of God's grace and mercy. 20 years of triumph and achievement. 20 years of soul-winning and fruit-bearing.

I rejoice in Christ my choice. We have sought to "win the lost at any cost." By His grace we are winners!

39

EWK

Never Be Negative

Philippians 4:13 is God's message to you today. "I can do all things through Christ who strengtheneth me."

You become one of those who can do all things, anything that He wishes done. His command means that His ability goes with the command.

Don't imprison yourself with negations and "I cant's."

Break absolutely free from the past that has mold and rot around it. Come into a new present, a new day, with the ability of God backing you.

Sing it: "God is at work within me. God and I can put it over. The Spirit of reality is making the things real in my heart."

Say it over and over again and your whole being will be flooded with light. The Word will become a living thing in your lips and you will be able to pray with the consciousness that you are reaching the throne, and that you are getting the thing for which you are praying.

Don't wait for a better education or more training, use what you have now.

Let the Word of Christ dwell in you richly, mastering everything that you undertake.

Have a positive testimony. Let it be your daily confession that "My God does supply every need of mine" . . . financially, spiritually, intellectually.

Let the world know that He has blessed you with every spiritual blessing right now, and that you are enjoying a present tense contact with Him.

Ephesians 3:20 is yours. "He is able to do exceeding abundantly above all that we ask or think, according to the power that worketh in us."

Let God loose in you. He has been imprisoned. You have made Him a little God, when He is the Creator God.

You have robbed Him of His initiative. You have silenced Him when He would speak.

You have held to your own weakness and failure, when His strength was awaiting your command.

You have talked failure. You have talked sickness. You have talked negatively when you should have been positive.

You should have said firmly, "I know in whom I have put my trust. I know He is able, with exceeding ability to make me a success. I have the ability of God within me."

SAY IT OUT LOUD. SAY IT OVER AND OVER AGAIN.

Psalm 23, "Jehovah is now my shepherd. I do not want. He is leading me into the riches of His grace, into the fullness of His blessing."

Psalm 27:1, "Jehovah is my light and my salvation; who shall I fear, Jehovah is the strength of my life: of whom shall I be afraid?"

Jehovah there is Jesus. The Lord of whom He is speaking is the One who gave Himself up for you.

He loves you now and longs to put you over and make you a success. He is, right now, your present help. It makes no difference what your environment is, what your troubles are. He is bigger.

It doesn't make any difference what your limitations are or what the disease in your body is, or your lack of money.

God is in the room there with you now. He is there with His Omnipotence. He is there with His perfect wisdom. He is there with healing and victory for you. Thank Him for it. Tell Him that you are glad He is with you.

John 14:23, "If a man love me, he will keep my word: and my Father will love him, and We will come unto him, and make Our abode with him."

He is there with you now.

Give Him a place, honour Him. Thank Him for His presence. Thank Him for His ability.

Thank Him that you are done with past failures, that you are living now in the light of victory.

When I Don't Feel Like It

Mark 11:23, '"*He shall have whatsoever he saith.*"

What I say is what I get. What I confess is what I possess. My confession of the Word precedes my possession of the promises of God's Word. Matthew 4:4, "Man shall not live by bread alone, but by every word that proceedeth from the mouth of God." Realizing I get what I say, I let the Word of God prevail and have free course. I endeavor to speak the Word only (Matthew 8:8).

When I need healing, I speak aloud as often as possible. "By His stripes I am healed" I Peter 2:24. I say it when I feel like saying it. I say it especially when I don't feel like saying it. When sharp pain strikes my body. I say it. When I awaken in the middle of the night with symptoms of some ailment, I say it. I say it when I arise in the morning, and I say it when I retire at night. I say it with all the confidence

I can muster. I say it when I have no confidence at all. I say it. I say it. I say it. Isaiah 53:5, "With His stripes I am healed."

When I am weak, I break the silence by saying Psalm 27:1, "The Lord is the strength of my life," and Philippians 4:13, "I can do all things through Christ who strengtheneth me." Yes, I say it when I feel well and strong. But especially I say it when I feel weak and defeated. I say it when I am on the mountain top of spiritual blessing: I say it especially when I am away down in the valley of melancholy and despair.

When I am fearful, I speak with authority II Timothy 1:7, "God hath not given me the spirit of fear, but of power, of love, and of a sound mind." I loosen up and speak up, and my fears vanish. Feeling or no feeling, I know the Lord liveth and abideth and my stand is upon that sure Rock.

When I am tempted to doubt God's Word: I doubt that doubt; doubt is of the devil and God classifies me as a believer. If I believe, I receive; if I doubt, I do without. I speak with bold assurance Romans 12:3, "God hath dealt to every man the measure of faith." Faith is something that I have, for God hath given to every man the measure of faith. Faith is what I actually believe in the very depths of my heart.

When I lack money, I speak these seven

words, "My God shall supply all my need" Philippians 4:19. I say it when I have money in the bank and I say it when my bank account is flat. I say it when my senses register that I am prospering, and I say it when it appears I am poverty-stricken. When I live by the Word, two grand promises assure me of these results: Psalm 1:3, "Whatsoever he doeth shall prosper;" Joshua 1:8, "Thou shalt make thy way prosperous, and thou shalt have good success."

Morning, noon and night and somewhere in between, I speak God's Word. This is the greatest self-discipline in which I will ever be engaged: to speak God's Word at all times, under all circumstances. I think God's Word in silence, then I speak it aloud as often as possible. I say it when the pressure from the enemy is upon me. And I say it when I am basking in the ecstacies of the Spirit! I say it when I feel like saying it. Especially I say it when I don't feel like saying it!

"Ye Are of God"

Ye are of God." This is the believer.

Speaking of another class of people he says "They are of the world, therefore speak they as of the world."

But we are of God. "Except a man is born from above, born of the spirit, born of the Word he cannot enter the kingdom of God."

We have received God's nature and life and ability.

With His nature we receive the characteristics of God. If we fellowship with Him we acquire the habits of God that we see in Jesus in His earth walk.

We learn the language of heaven so that the Word as it contacts us becomes a part of us.

I John 4:4, "Ye are of God my little children and have overcome them." Linger about that expression, "have overcome them."

The work has been accomplished. When Jesus overcame the adversary, you were with Him. It was your victory.

Now He is telling us that we are overcomers.

I John 2:14, "I have written unto you young men because you are strong and the Word of God abideth in you and you have overcome the evil one."

They overcame in their present day combat through the Word that was living in them.

The Word is God's voice, God speaking to us. It is a part of Himself. It is God in us who has overcome the evil one. The forces that were arrayed against us were brought into subjection, into captivity.

"They overcame him by the word of their testimony." That is the Logos, the Word of God.

We are conquerors today by our testimony.

It is our testimony which wins. We conquer the adversary with our testimony, our confession of faith.

We declare that the spirit that raised Jesus from the dead, and who is dwelling in us has healed our bodies, given strength and clearness to our thinking, made us victors where defeat had reigned for years.

Now He says, "And have overcome them." Why? "Because greater is He that is in you than he that is in the world."

The greater One is in us.

I like to think that the Holy Spirit did not lay aside any of His ability or wisdom or might when He made His home in the believer's body.

He can use the sword of the Spirit through our lips and conquer every force.

We overcome by the Word in our lips.

The Name of Jesus in your lips becomes as mighty as the words that fell from the lips of Jesus when He walked on earth.

We haven't realized it.

We did not realize that the Word of Christ in our lips was just like the words falling from the lips of the Master.

It has been hard for us to accept the fact that His Word is a living thing in the lips of the believer.

It has comfort and consolation for the heart. It has power and authority in the lips.

You face life unafraid, you face life a conqueror.

My Never Again List

Never again will I confess "I can't" for "I can do all things through Christ which strengtheneth me" Philippians 4:13.

Never again will I confess lack, for "My God shall supply all my need according to His riches in glory by Christ Jesus" Philippians 4:19.

Never again will I confess fear, for "God hath not given me the spirit of fear, but of power, and of love, and of a sound mind" II Timothy 1:7.

Never again will I confess doubt and lack of faith, for "God hath given to every man the measure of faith" Romans 12:3.

Never again will I confess weakness, for "The Lord is the strength of my life" Psalm 27:1, and "The people that know their God shall be strong and do exploits" Daniel 11:32.

Never again will I confess supremacy of Satan over my life, for "Greater is He that is within me than he that is in the world" I John 4:4.

Never again will I confess defeat, for "God always causeth me to triumph in Christ Jesus" II Corinthians 2:14.

Never again will I confess lack of wisdom, for "Christ Jesus is made unto me wisdom from God" I Corinthians 1:30.

Never again will I confess sickness, for "with His stripes I am healed" Isaiah 53:5, and Jesus "Himself took my infirmities and bare my sickness" Matthew 8:17.

Never again will I confess worries and frustrations, for I am "Casting all my cares upon Him who careth for me" I Peter 5:7. In Christ I am "Care-free!"

Never again will I confess bondage, for "Where the Spirit of the Lord is, there is liberty" II Corinthians 3:17. My body is the temple of the Holy Spirit!

Never again will I confess condemnation, for "There is therefore now no condemnation to them which are in Christ Jesus" Romans 8:1. I am in Christ; therefore, I am free from condemnation.

Never again will I confess loneliness. Jesus said, "Lo, I am with you always, even unto the end of the world" Matthew 28:20 and "I will never leave thee, nor forsake thee" Hebrews 13:5.

Never again will I confess curses and bad luck, for, "Christ hath redeemed us from the curse of the law, being made a curse for us: that the blessing of Abraham might come on the Gentiles through Jesus Christ; that we might receive the promise of the Spirit through faith" Galatians 3:13-14.

Never again will I confess discontent because "I have learned, in whatsoever state (circumstance) I am, therewith to be content" Philippians 4:11.

Never again will I confess unworthiness because "He hath made Him to be sin for us, who knew no sin; that we might be made the righteousness of God in Him" II Corinthians 5:21.

Never again will I confess confusion because "God is not the author of confusion, but of peace" I Corinthians 14:33, and "We have received not the spirit of the world, but the Spirit which is of God, that we might know the things that are freely given to us of God" I Corinthians 2:12.

Never again will I confess persecution, for "If God be for us, who can be against us?" Romans 8:31.

Never again will I confess the dominion of sin over my life because "The law of the Spirit of life in Christ Jesus hath made me free from the law of sin and death" Romans 8:2, and "As far as the east is from the west, so far hath He removed our transgressions from us" Psalm 103:12.

Never again will I confess insecurity because "When thou liest down, thou shalt not be afraid; yea, thou shalt lie down, and thy sleep shall be sweet . . . for the Lord shall be thy confidence, and shall keep thy foot from being taken" Proverbs 3:24-26.

Never again will I confess failure because, "Nay, in all these things we are more than conquerors through Him that loved us" Romans 8:37.

Never again will I confess frustration, for "Thou wilt keep him in perfect peace, whose mind is stayed on thee: because he trusteth in thee" Isaiah 26:3.

Never again will I confess fear of the future, "But as it is written, eye hath not seen, nor ear heard, neither have entered into the heart of man, the things which God hath prepared for them that love Him, but God hath revealed them unto us by His Spirit" I Corinthians 2:9-10.

Never again will I confess troubles because Jesus said, "In the world ye shall have tribula-

tion: but be of good cheer; I have overcome
the world" John 16:33.

Faith Exercise

Talk the Way You Would Like To Be and You Will Be the Way You Talk

You confess Jesus as Lord "unto salvation" Romans 10:10. You confess Him first, then God acts to recreate your spirit. This Speaking Forth Principle is clearly seen in scripture. "Even God, who quickeneth the dead, and calleth those things which be not as though they were" Romans 4:17. God spoke the Word first, then His acts of creation came into being. You speak, then you possess. You talk the way you would like to be and you will be the way you talk.

"That the communication of thy faith may become effectual, by the acknowledging of every good thing which is in you in Christ Jesus" Philemon 6. Your faith becomes effectual by your acknowledging or speaking forth every good thing in you in Christ Jesus. You speak, then reality comes.

"We then also having the same spirit of

faith, according as it is written, I believed, therefore have I spoken; we also believe, therefore do we speak" II Corinthians 4:13. In order for your faith to be activated, you speak forth!

Do you desire to be healthy? Then speak the healthgiving scriptures. When you talk the Word, Proverbs 4:22 assures that this Word-living process will produce "health to all your flesh." Talk about it, "I have a healthy mind, healthy eyes, nose, mouth, heart, blood vessels, nerves, bones, organs." When you have a health problem, speak to that mountain, Jesus declared, and you "shall have whatsoever you say" (Mark 11:23).

Do you desire to be a strong Christian? "Let the weak say, I am strong" Joel 3:10. It is not the strong who affirms he is strong, but the weak. It is talk first, then you become in reality. That's the faith way to please God.

Do you desire to be a loving person? Then talk that way because "the love of God is shed abroad in your heart by the Holy Ghost" Romans 5:5. Do you desire to be successful? Then speak success. Do you wish to be bold in Christ? Then talk boldly for "the righteous are bold as a lion" Proverbs 28:1.

Tributes
to
E.W. Kenyon
and
Don Gossett

43
EWK

"There Came a Man Sent from God"

By Rev. Jack Mitchell

In 1931 a stranger came to us here in the great Pacific Northwest bringing a message of love. He preached a message of One who loved us and gave Himself up to die for us that we might come into the family of the great Father God. He brought the message of Redemption, of healing and of righteousness. Through his ministry reality came to our hungry hearts.

For years his early morning broadcasts over the radio enriched the lives of multitudes. Many heard his cheery "Good morning" to the radio announcer and then "Good morning friends of radio-land, so happy to be with you again."

Many who never attended church were reached for Christ through those broadcasts. In visiting a small farm in the south end I heard the testimony of a farmer and his wife who stopped their morning chores to listen to the broadcast each morning. Their hearts were drawn by the message of love and finally won to the Lord Jesus Christ. Words could not express what those messages from the heart of the Father meant to them.

Gratitude fills our hearts for his faithfulness in presenting to us what God had given to him. The spiritual enrichment through a greater knowledge of God's Word has indeed endeared to our hearts the man through which that light came. To some of us the borders of the Kingdom of heaven were extended. Once we were outside, now we are fellow members of that great eternal kingdom that cannot be shaken.

He has gone to be with his Lord, to enjoy the glories of heaven. He leaves behind vast God-given treasures of spiritual blessings for us to enjoy while he goes to the sure reward that awaits the faithful minister. I count it a rare privilege to have known him and to have had the joy of his fellowship. May the Lord bless his memory to your hearts.

44

EWK

The Faith Builder
By Rev. Carl Olson

I came in contact with the ministry of Dr. Kenyon by hearing him over the radio. It was my privilege to be directly or indirectly under his ministry for some ten years.

Dr. Kenyon had a long and fruitful ministry of over fifty years, and he will live on in the hearts of those who knew him and in the literature which he labored so hard to leave in the hands of posterity.

I am sure that the Lord welcomed his coming as one of His great Generals in the Faith. Paul wrote to Timothy, "Fight the good fight of Faith," and again, "Be ye a good soldier of the Lord Jesus Christ," and "Well done, thou good and faithful servant—enter thou into the joy of the Lord."

Dr. Kenyon was known as a teacher of teachers. Over the air he was known as "The Faith Builder." Through his ministry of the Word men and women were made pleasing to God. What a challenge that is to every Christian worker. Many a young minister and worker has been given a start, inspiration and encouragement through the friendly advice and counsel of Dr. Kenyon. He knew the secret of a successful ministry. He was an early riser, and through his communion with the Lord he was able to help and build others up. He had love and encouragement for all. The only enemy he recognized was the devil and his helpers. But he knew how to deal with them in the Name of our Lord Jesus Christ.

Dr. Kenyon knew the secret of Divine Love. He loved men and women into the Kingdom of God, and then built the Word into them so they could stand victoriously. It was Dr. Kenyon who said, "I would rather die than be a failure. You are a success because you are tied up with the omnipotence. God never made a failure. You have the life of God. You have His ability and strength."

Dr. Kenyon was a master of words. To me he was the most forceful and powerful speaker that I have ever witnessed behind the pulpit. His messages from the Word of God were always fresh and packed with Divine Dynamite.

He was a pioneer in radio work on the West coast. This ministry has had a far reaching effect on the Church. Thousands here in the

Northwest and millions the world over through his writings, have felt the impact of this man's ministry. Truly he was a great ambassador for the Lord Jesus Christ.

Dr. Kenyon was a faithful minister of the Word of God. He was never known to be late for an appointment or service. His faith-building messages from the Lord were unique and definitely for these last days. We who were personally acquainted with Dr. Kenyon appreciate the Word more and more which he opened to us.

45

EWK

The Ministry of Dr. E.W. Kenyon

By Don Gossett

In 1952, I was ministering with Evangelist
William Freeman in the State of California.
A lady evangelist, Daisy Wiltbanks, gave me a
copy of the book, *The Wonderful Name of Jesus*,
written by E.W. Kenyon.

This was my first introduction to the writings of Dr. Kenyon. Because the Holy Spirit
had given me a personal revelation of the power
and authority of the Name of Jesus the previous
year, it was with great anticipation that I began
to read this book. When I say I read it, I literally devoured it. Day after day, I would read,
meditate and then put into practise the authority of the Name of Jesus. Almost every waking
minute was devoted to Jesus, and the wonder
of His Name.

After I read this book, I wrote to Dr. Kenyon at the address inside to inquire if he had
written other books. For some time I had no

reply to the letter. I then tried to call long distance to Seattle, Washington, the city of his address. The operator informed me there was no listing for E. W. Kenyon. I decided that this would likely be my only contact with this man and his ministry: the book, *The Wonderful Name of Jesus.*

Within two weeks, however, a letter did come from the Kenyon Gospel Publishing Society, with a new address in Fullerton, California. The letter was from Dr. Kenyon's daughter, Ruth, advising me that her father had been promoted to heaven, that she was carrying on his ministry. She then told me about many of the books he had written. I placed an order for all of them.

One by one, I continued reading these tremendous books. All of my young ministry I had been an eager reader of most of the leading evangelical and full gospel authors. Suddenly, I was aware that my ministry was being influenced in an overwhelming manner by the writings of Dr. Kenyon. The way he presented the Word with such revelation of the Holy Spirit, the clarity of his thought, his challenges to act upon the Word, this was revolutionary beyond any writings I'd ever read.

In 1956, I was again in California for evangelistic meetings. I made a trip to Fullerton to visit Ruth Kenyon and her mother, the wife of Dr. Kenyon. Our fellowship was so sweet. I have cherished the memory of that initial personal meeting with the Kenyons. We talked for hours about how Dr. Kenyon gave himself day and night to the study of the Word, how he constantly walked in the Spirit, and the treasury of truth he left behind.

In every corner of the world I have travelled, I have met those whose lives have been transformed by the writings of E. W. Kenyon. I'm so glad that I was privileged to come in contact with his ministry. I have continued to enjoy rich fellowship with Ruth and other family members through the years.

46
EWK

My Dad, Dr. E.W. Kenyon

By His Daughter, Ruth

Dad was born in Saratoga County, New York the fourth son of a family of ten. When he was in his teens, the family moved to Amsterdam, New York, in the Mohawk Valley. He grew up in Amsterdam, studied at Amsterdam Academy, and at the age of 19 preached his first sermon in the Methodist Church there.

From his earliest days, Dad had a thirst for knowledge, and what he learned he wanted to pass on to others. That desire for study was the driving force in his life. When a young boy, he felt the call to the ministry and though he had to go to work in the carpet mills as a weaver at the age of 15, every spare minute was devoted to study.

He worked his way through school, attended various schools in New Hampshire and Emerson College of Oratory in Boston, Massachusetts. Always he had one fixed goal . . . to preach the gospel, to "study to show thyself approved unto God, a workman that needeth not to be ashamed, handling aright the Word of truth." II Timothy 2:15.

He was pastor of several churches in the New England States; at the age of thirty he founded and was president of Bethel Bible Institute at Spencer, Massachusetts. (This school was later moved to Providence, Rhode Island and is known as Providence Bible Institute).

Through his ministry at Bethel, hundreds of young men and women were trained and ordained for the ministry, and are now out preaching the Word in all parts of the world.

For over twenty years he traveled in evangelistic work in the East, and was known far and wide. Thousands were saved and healed in these services.

After he left the East, he came to California where he also traveled in evangelistic work. He was pastor of a church in Los Angeles for several years and was one of the pioneers of radio work on the Pacific Coast.

In 1931 he came to the Northwest, and for many years his morning broadcast, "Kenyon's Church of the Air," was an inspiration and blessing to thousands.

He founded "The New Covenant Baptist Church" here in Seattle, and for many years was its pastor.

During the busy years of his ministry he found time to write and publish fourteen books, hundreds of poems and songs (some of which have never been published), correspondence courses and tracts. At the time of his death he had material assembled for twelve additional books, and one was ready for publication. He left hundreds of articles and sermons which have never yet been published.

Shortly before his passing he had a premonition that he would not be here long, and he called me and said he felt I was the one to carry on his work. He said, "Ruth, dear, I have a feeling I won't be with you much longer. This work must go on. It is up to you now. You have been looking after it all these years, and with the help of the Lord, I know you can carry on." I promised him I would.

This work which he started has continued to bless untold thousands as it has in the past. Our work is now reaching to all corners of the world. Our circulation has increased greatly. There has never been a time when the world needed this message as it does now.

Don Gossett: A Daughter's Perspective

By Judy Gossett

This morning while watching television, I observed several famous contemporary evangelists: Oral Roberts, Rex Humbard and Robert Schuller. It was quite interesting to note the participation and support of their children in their respective ministries. It seems as though a chief accomplishment for each of these great men was to have their own flesh and blood actively involved with them, endorsing them, believing in and wholeheartedly supporting the work God has called their fathers to.

On behalf of the five Gossett children, I want to pay tribute to our father, Don Gossett.

One of the most striking memories I carry from childhood is we seven Gossetts—Dad, Mom, Michael, Jeanne, Donnie, Marisa and me—packed into our blue '56 Buick, driving from one city to the next in our evangelistic travels. As we grew restless and tired of playing our children's games in the tight quarters of our old car, Dad would announce, "Okay, kids, it's Bible story time!" As Dad recounted thrilling stories from the Old and New Testament, we became mesmerized by each event and character, feeling sure that at any moment, Moses would put in a cameo appearance, complete with the Ten Commandments in hand! Or that we were trekking the water beside Peter as Jesus directed! These were fascinating, vibrant stories which we devoured.

Bible quizzes, 'sword drills' and scripture memorization followed Bible story time. We children preferred the time spent in the Word with our parents to any other activity of our journeys. Thankfully, many times the Lord has brought to my remembrance the scriptures and lessons learned in those long hours in our car. These have been invaluable in building the spiritual character and witness needed to be effective for Christ.

Because we traveled so much, it was difficult for us to establish long-term relationships with the people we met. As a result, our family grew closer than ever.

Many afternoons outside our motel room, we played sports: lively games of baseball and touch football or rivaled each other in endurance-testing races and swimming. Usually, in the middle of the jovial festivities was our favourite competitor and coach: Dad.

In spite of the deep love and devotion in our family, it seemed as though we were constantly plagued with near-poverty, sickness, mediocrity and frustration.

Then in 1961, we moved back to Canada and the Lord turned around Dad's ministry. God showed Dad the power of Jesus' name coupled with the positive confession of the Word and joyful praise were the keys to success and victorious living. These truths revolutionized our lives! We could never again live in the defeatism of past years in the ministry.

As we grew older, Dad and Mother experienced more problems with us as teenagers. However, they never shirked from these obstacles, but always met them head-on with these responses: discipling, the Word, the Name of Jesus and prayer. Michael, Jeanne, Donnie, Marisa and I aren't perfect, but we do possess a wonderful heritage from our confident-through-Christ, persevering parents. And now with Jeanne's children, Jennifer and Alexander, another generation is receiving these same truths we were taught years ago.

These have been exciting years for Dad's ministry! The Lord opened the doors for the Bold Living radio broadcasts to beam into 89 countries. God increased Dad's visibility as an author and gave him more than 80 books to publish. We opened offices in both Canada and the States to service the needs of the partners God raised up to support the various outreaches of the ministry. Dad has gone overseas more than 40 times to spread the good news of Jesus' love with those who have never heard.

Perhaps you have always heard of Don Gossett as evangelist. Radio speaker. Administrator. Author. Missionary.

By way of this brief personal glimpse, I hope you know him a little better as compassionate man of God. Loving father. Proud grandfather. And my wonderful friend.

ABOUT DON GOSSETT

For more than fifty years, Don Gossett has been serving the Lord through full-time ministry. Born again at the age of twelve, Don answered his call to the ministry just five years later, beginning by reaching out to his unsaved family members. In March 1948, Don overcame his longtime fear of public speaking and began his ministry in earnest, preaching for two country Baptist churches in Oklahoma.

Blessed with the gift of writing, Don became editor of the Bible College magazine in San Francisco; afterward, he was invited to become editor of an international magazine. Following this, he served as editor of T. L. Osborn's *Faith Digest*, a magazine that reached over 600,000 homes each month. Don apprenticed with many well-known evangelists, beginning with William Freeman, one of America's leading healing evangelists during the late 1940s. He also spent time with Jack Coe and Raymond T. Richey.

Don has penned many works, particularly ones on the power of the spoken word and praise. His writings have been translated into almost twenty languages and have exceeded twenty-five million in worldwide distribution. Additionally, Don has also recorded scores of audio series. His daily radio broadcast, launched in 1961, has been released into eighty-nine nations worldwide.

Don raised five children with his first wife, Joyce, who died in 1991. In 1995, Don found lifelong love again and married Debra, an anointed teacher of the Word. They have ministered worldwide and have lived in British Columbia, Canada, and in Blaine, Washington State.

About E. W. Kenyon

Born in Saratoga county, New York, E. W. Kenyon (1867–1948) moved with his family to Amsterdam, New York, when he was in his teens. Kenyon studied at Amsterdam Academy, and, at the age of nineteen, preached his first sermon in the Methodist church there.

He worked his way through school, attending various schools in New Hampshire, as well as Emerson College of Oratory in Boston, Massachusetts.

Kenyon served as pastor of several churches in the New England states. At the age of thirty, he founded and became president of Bethel Bible Institute in Spencer, Massachusetts. (This school was later moved to Providence, Rhode Island, and is known as Providence Bible Institute.) Through his ministry at Bethel, hundreds of young men and women were trained and ordained for the ministry.

After traveling throughout the Northeast preaching the gospel and seeing the salvation and healing of thousands, Kenyon moved to California, where he continued his evangelistic travels. He was pastor of a church in Los Angeles for several years and was one of the pioneers of radio work on the Pacific Coast.

In 1931, he moved to the Northwest, and for many years his morning broadcast, *Kenyon's Church of the Air*, was an inspiration and blessing to thousands. He also founded the New Covenant Baptist Church in Seattle, where he pastored for many years.

During the busy years of his ministry, he found time to write and publish sixteen books, as well as many correspondence courses and tracts, and he composed hundreds of poems and songs. The work that he started has continued to bless untold thousands.